Wine tasting / enjoying / understanding

Wine tasting enjoying understanding

Michael Broadbent MW

New and revised edition: 1977

Christie's Wine Publications

Editorial adviser: Edmund Penning-Rowsell

Christie's Wine Publications
Editor Michael Broadbent, M.W.
Editorial adviser Edmund Penning-Rowsell
8 King Street, St. James's, London, SW1, England

Wine Tasting
First published in 1968 by Wine & Spirit Publications Ltd
Second edition 1970
Third revised edition by Christie Wine Publications 1973
Fourth revised and enlarged edition 1975, reprinted 1976
Special reprint for Findlater Mackie Todd & Co. Ltd. 1976
Special reprint for Dreyfus Ashby, New York 1977
Fifth revised edition 1977

French translation by Baron Geoffroy de Luze published in serial form
by *La Revue du Vin de France* 1970/1

Italian translation by Count Riccardo Riccardi published in serial form
by *Gourmet Club* of Milan 1972/3

Danish edition, translation by Kay Nielsen, published by Chr. Ericksens
Forlag, Copenhagen 1975

German edition, translation by Hanspeter Reichmuth, published by Raeber,
Luzern and Stuttgart 1976

ISBN 0 903432 11 0

design/print in England by
Eyre & Spottiswoode Ltd, Queen's Printers,
Thanet Press, Margate, Kent

Contents

Foreword to the 2nd edition

Michael Broadbent and I have long and pleasant wine associations. In his early days I was his immediate boss and although he had already, as it were, fluttered out of the 'wine nest', he was still something of a fledgling. Since then, with innate skill, intelligence and hard work, he has reached his present eminent position in wine circles and it is abundantly clear that he will continue to rise to greater heights. All these attributes are enhanced by a musical ear and considerable aptitude for drawing and painting. Undoubtedly, it is precisely those talents which have aided his career in the art of wine.

If one may judge from the surprising number of books published about wine every year, there must be quite a number of people who are forming a small library on the subject. Now Michael's book is different from the rest; instead of being a rehash of what has so often been written before, it gets down to the basic facts of how to taste and smell and assess every wine as you drink it – invaluable aid to the aspiring connoisseur. Although in our youth pains are taken to instruct us in the arts in general, virtually nothing is done to develop the 'poor relations' of the senses, those of taste and smell. Hence, our low standard of gastronomy. In France, the children are taught to appreciate basic good cooking at home and so when they grow up they are not prepared to tolerate, for instance, bad fare in a restaurant. In England we are not sufficiently discriminating.

This lack of discrimination also applies to wine, and with the current flood of rather indifferent 'popular' wines on the market, there is some danger that we will lose, or never develop, our senses of appreciation and discernment. *Wine Tasting* – in a new and slightly extended edition now, I am pleased to see – does more than point out these dangers; it helps combat them by demonstrating how to develop a God-given attribute with which most of us are blessed, a sense of taste which, once developed, should help to make our daily lives more agreeable.

H. H. WAUGH
London, February 1970

Introduction

Most authors . . . in sending forth a work that has any pretensions to novelty, endeavour to conciliate the favour of their readers, by acknowledging the rashness of the enterprise and expatiating on the difficulties which they have encountered in the execution of it. These excuses, it is true, are seldom sincere . . . HENDERSON, A History of Ancient & Modern Wines, 1824.

New approach to new edition

The introduction to the first edition of my book explained how the book arose and mentioned some of those who, often unknown to themselves, had exerted an influence. The quotation above, from Henderson's pioneer work on wine, was singularly appropriate. A battery of Forewords gave me moral support.

Now, after running through several editions and reprints, some in translation, and having been read in one form or another by a remarkably large number of people in many countries, I feel less inclined to burden readers with apologies and, as Edmund Penning-Rowsell wrote in a revision copy, 'Let's cut the cackle and open the bottle!'

What I propose to do is to explain the form of the book and suggest how it best be used.

As the origin and development of *Wine Tasting* is relevant I have retained a brief account of the background of the work, but the acknowledgements have been augmented and listed in a new appendix.

Background

The original article, upon which this handbook is based, was written in 1962. At the time, I was with Harveys of Bristol, and one of my tasks was to conduct weekly tastings for the executives and sales staff. What struck me then was not only the inconsistency of the approach to tasting in general but that, understandably, the newer recruits had very little idea what to look for when confronted by an unknown glass of wine. As for laymen, the vast majority had not the faintest idea how to proceed – this was immediately apparent at the many lecture-tastings that I, and other members of the Harvey staff, conducted all over the country in those days. In short, very few seemed to know even the first principles of tasting. Nor were they helped by existing writers upon wine, for in the whole course of some pretty voracious reading I had come across not a book, or a chapter even, which – in English at any rate – dealt with what I considered a pretty vital subject.

Original pamphlet

So I wrote, more or less at one sitting, a paper headed *Guidance in the Technique of Tasting*. I showed this rather diffidently to my vice-chairman, who promptly suggested that it might be worthy of publication. I posted it to the editor of the monthly *Wine and Spirit Trade Record* (now *Wine and Spirit*) and, to my delight, it was accepted and published in several parts beginning in the June 1963 issue. If the late Hector King saw me into print, it was Kathleen Bourke who, the same year, gave it a wider audience through the medium of *Wine Magazine*. At the same

time, and under the same title, it was printed as a training handbook
for the Harveys of Bristol Group of Companies.

Cyril Ray commissioned a revised version for the 1964 edition of
The Compleat Imbiber; Watney's, the brewers, printed a version of the
Harveys handbook for the training of their own wine department staff,
and sections were reprinted elsewhere, even in Swedish.

In book form

By this time I felt that there was enough evidence of interest to expand
the notes and publish them in book form, so, with Kathleen Bourke's
assistance and encouragement, *Wine Tasting* appeared under the imprint
of *Wine and Spirit Publications* in December 1968, then revised and
enlarged again in 1973, as one of Christie's monographs.

Foreign editions

My old friend Geoffroy de Luze of Bordeaux did a French translation
of the original which was published, serialised, in *La Revue du Vin
de France* (1970/1), and Riccardo Riccardi nobly did the same in Italian
for *Gourmet Club* of Milan (1972/3). The first translation published in
book form was Danish, by Chr. Erichsens Forlag, in 1975. Hanspeter
Reichmuth worked on a more up-to-date edition for German readers and
the book *Weine – prüfen, kennen, geniessen* appeared simultaneously in
Switzerland and Germany last autumn. A Dutch translation is being
prepared at the moment, and a charming Japanese lady, working for a great
far-eastern trading company, is bravely attempting a translation to be
published in Tokyo.

**Approach to
tasting**

If all this gives me some pleasure and satisfaction, it also concerns me
lest it should even remotely be considered the last word on the subject,
whereas it was originally intended to be a 'first word', encouraging beginners
to begin, pointing them in the right direction. I confess I also try to
illuminate the darker corners, to put elements in perspective, for those
who already know quite a bit about the subject. But, as Pamela Vandyke
Price observes: '. . . there are other methods and approaches'.

Above all, though, it is method and order I preach, and conciseness
of expression I try to encourage. It is possible to taste without talking,
but not to communicate without words.

Contents

As readers will have gathered, the book has grown from the rather
unadorned original that dealt with the 'technique' of tasting and the
organisation of tastings, to the working of the senses, the elements that
give rise to taste, the characteristics of wines and districts. All this has
led irrevocably to the latest chapter, 'The Use of Words', that bridges
the gap between the actions of tasting and the glossary. The latter
I regard as significant, for as this is a *book* about tasting, the words used
throughout have been chosen carefully. Yorkshire-born, I hate waste,
so directness, 'lack of cant' as someone put it, and conciseness and
absence of padding are what make this, even enlarged and revised, a
handbook rather than a coffee-table puff book.

Brought up in a consumer- rather than producer-country, and with my
training being as a retail wine merchant and not an oenologist, my language

is as straightforward and non-technical as I can make it: in lecturing **and** writing I have always tried to bear the enthusiastic *amateur* in mind.

How to use the book

If you are a beginner, I suggest you read chapters I, II and III in order and then jump to V, VI and VII. If you are learning the business, start at chapter II, then V, VI, VII, back to IV and then on to XI and XII and appendix i. For further reading, I hope the book-list will be of help.

Keen amateurs and members of wine clubs and societies will, I trust, find chapter X useful (even experienced organisers of tastings find the check list on page 82 useful); and seasoned tasters might like to read, and argue with me about, chapters VIII and IX.

Acknowledgements

One of the best things about wine is the bond it creates between people of like mind. Those who grow and make it are extraordinarily kind and hospitable; those who deal in it, with only a few exceptions, display a deeper than commercial attachment. And those who merely love wine as one of the minor pleasures of life always appear to be the most civilised of people.

Thanks . . .

Over the past quarter of a century I have benefited, as have others, to a quite immeasurable extent from the generosity of growers, shippers and merchants. Equally, I have to thank those many individuals, clubs and societies with whom I have been privileged to share their private and collective treasures.

Since this book was first published, and arising out of the nature of my job, tasting opportunities have multiplied. Indeed my 'exposure' to fine and rare wines, through tastings in old cellars and at Christie's, through travelling, dining, lecturing (and auctioning) far and wide, places me in an enviable and somewhat invidious position; for I can never adequately repay hosts, friends, clients – all the providers of tasting opportunities. What I can do is to pass on my experiences, and to acknowledge unusual and memorable kindnesses by naming names in an appendix towards the end of the book.

I hope that the following chapters will awaken an interest in tasting, help in the approach, and make the more experienced tasters think harder about the methods and words they use; and that they may encourage those teetering on the brink to plunge into the unfathomable depths of wine.

MICHAEL BROADBENT
*London, SW*1
Autumn 1977

I: The approach to tasting

I was convinced forty years ago – and the conviction remains to this day – that in wine tasting and wine-talk there is an enormous amount of humbug.
T. G. SHAW Wine, the Vine and the Cellar, 1863

Basic approach

It is not necessary to know all about the internal combustion engine in order to drive a car. It is, however, generally agreed that driving lessons are essential and, in the final analysis, practice makes perfect. In the same way, a detailed knowledge of viniculture and viticulture is not a prerequisite for the enjoyment of wine, though an understanding of basic principles, some experience and a moderately discerning palate are essential if wine is to be appreciated as something more than an ordinary drink.

Ability to taste

If one can taste food, one can taste wine. Generally speaking what *is* good smells and tastes good; what smells 'off' and has a nasty taste is bad. I believe this is the reason for most people being able, correctly, to place one wine better than another simply on the basis that it tastes or smells nicer: that elementary 'hedonistic' judgment will fairly accurately pin down the relative quality of the wines in question. Saying *why* one is better than another is a different matter. There are however exceptions to the above rule: an over-mature wine, like an over-ripe cheese or well-hung game bird, sometimes has a putrid overtone to the smell and taste which can be unattractive, even repellent, to the uninitiated, though appreciated, sometimes sought after, by a connoisseur. It is all a matter of taste, *and* experience. Experience, as always, takes time; it cannot be bought or 'swotted up'.

First principles

But what about the first principles? Of all the books, articles and spoken words on the subject of wine, what number describe what the wine actually tastes like or indeed how to set about tasting it? In the course of some pretty voracious reading, up to the time I originally wrote the book, I had come across not a book, hardly a chapter, which – at any rate in English – deals with what I considered a pretty basic subject: taste. This is not to say that background information about districts, soil, grape varieties, wine making and wine makers is not interesting or valuable; indeed, later chapters deal with the influence of such elements on taste. The history of wine, of firms and people, add to one's awareness, but such vital fringe activities are apt to obscure the main object of the exercise which is the appreciation of wine: its colour, bouquet and flavour. Over the past year or so there has been a positive spate of attempts, more and less successful, to deal with the subject. The French, in particular, seem to be making up for lost time – and I suggest books on the subject, Appendix V. There are, of course, difficulties in getting down to brass tacks. Tasting is subjective, and the language needed for describing wine smells and flavours is singularly ill-defined and anything but universally accepted. What perhaps is needed is something approaching musical notation, for in many ways the problems are similar. Both music and wine appeal to the senses, one of hearing and the other of taste and smell; both are fleeting, in the sense that actual sounds and flavours cannot be retained by the receptive ear or palate; both, on the other hand, can be appreciated, even greatly loved, by people who lack technical knowledge or who are without a deep interest. But to reach the heights of full understanding and to convey this to someone else rather more is required.

The first stage is an awareness of first principles, the second a detailed appreciation of what lies behind the colour, smell and taste of any wine; the third is plenty of practice.

Practice and memory

Although wine can be consumed with enjoyment without a lot of fuss and nonsense, *reasoned* judgment of the finer wines must be based on knowledge, and this can only be acquired by the sort of practice in tasting that will help a vinous memory – a memory that will hold in store the great touchstones, the standard norms and the exceptions to the rules.

There is no doubt that some people are endowed with a more delicate and sensitive palate than others, but this alone is less useful than a normal but well-trained and experienced palate. Mind you, a refined palate *and* an excellent memory will give a relatively new taster a head start. The greatest tasters will surely be those with all the physical attributes, wide experience and a flawless memory. In the end it is memory which lets one down, which is why it is advisable to make notes.

Perspective and common sense

The main thing is to keep tasting in perspective. To spend time and effort only on those wines that are worthy of attention; to talk intensely about wine only to those who are of like mind. In short don't get carried away; use a little common sense.

Above all, be true to yourself.

II: Why taste?

Tasting is the introduction of wine to our senses: sight, smell and taste.
EMILE PEYNAUD

**Tasting –
broad concept**

Wine is a beverage of enormous agricultural and commercial importance. Every drop of the millions of gallons made annually has one final objective: to be consumed. And, in passing the lips, crossing the tongue and descending the throat, wine is 'tasted', whether or not a conscious comment or judgment is made. However, the word 'tasting' in relation to wine refers to a deliberate, conscious and subjective act, the aim of which is to assess the qualities of the wine under review. Incidentally, the word 'tasting' is used here (as the French use *dégustation*) in the broader conventional sense, which I prefer to the more pedantic and academic terms 'sensory' and 'organoleptic' examinations.

Need to taste?

Does *all* wine need to be tasted in this sense? The answer is, no. For of the millions of gallons produced and marketed, by far the largest proportion is the plainest of ordinary beverage wine, made to be consumed as an adequate accompaniment to a meal or merely as a refreshing and restorative drink. This sort of wine is *not* made to be sipped reverently; nor is it meant to provide the basis of intellectual discussion. (It is immaterial that one of the end products of its consumption may be the mellowing of the drinkers and the loosening of their tongues to discuss *other* subjects with new enlightenment. Ordinary wine is for talking over, not talking about.)

Before finally dismissing plain, honest-to-goodness (one hopes) *vin de table*, a word about mass-produced wines may not come amiss.

**Oenology,
commerce and
mediocrity**

We are living in a world where, whether we like it or not, standards are concertina-ing. Thanks to new pesticides, new methods of controlling fermentation and other new techniques, less is now left to chance. Although fine vintages cannot be created artificially, certainly poor vintages are less disastrous than they used to be. This is a mixed blessing. If oenologists can rightly take credit for much of the improvement in the overall standard of wine making, they are also answerable for some of the decrease in character and individuality of 'fine wines' in certain classic areas. If more sound wine is made, then more is to be marketed; and the production of wine is as subject to the laws of supply and demand as any other commodity. Wine to be sold on a large scale has to be blended and, to be universally acceptable, has to be innocuous – which is a fortunate situation for the marketing man.

It is no coincidence that we live in the era of the 'light' and 'mild', subjected to a relatively new set of standards which apply to nearly all consumer products from 'mild-flavoured' cornflakes to 'light' whiskies. Unhappily, commercial necessity forces this pace, taking character and stuffing out of the raw material, reducing the awareness of the consumer to any elements of positive taste. What is not sufficiently realized is that mixing individual flavours has a similar effect to mixing colours: the more you mix, the greyer the result. Mass-marketed wines must be blended. Blended wines, of necessity and by design, lose much of their individuality and character and a 'grey' neutral wine often results. Neutral wines are inoffensive and therefore will not displease the majority. Which, unfortunately, is just one more example of how commercial necessity can become a marketing virtue.

Vital critical standards

It is in this context: to maintain interest and positive standards, that critical tasting must be kept alive. It would be a pity to allow man's finer perceptions of tasting experience (and resultant range of pleasures) to atrophy. Moreover, I do not think we should be obliged to 're-evaluate', i.e. lower, our standards in the light of technical 'improvements'.

Reasons for tasting

What, then, are the main reasons for tasting? The important thing to realize is that wine will be tasted throughout its life in different places, by different people and for a variety of practical reasons. Here are some of them:

☐ In the *chai* (*quinta, cantina,* whatever local name is given to the grower's cellar), the *maître de chai* or the proprietor will be acting as nurse and midwife. He will taste from the moment the *must* is fermented into wine, watching its condition, balance and development, until it is sold or bottled.

☐ The broker and the merchant prior to making a purchase will also taste from the grower's cask during this period. For the lay amateur, tasting young wine from a cask in a *chai* – such a romantic-sounding occupation – may be sadly disappointing. Few things can be so starkly raw and scouring as a mouthful of purple new wine. Much better to leave it at this stage to the professionals!

☐ Samples may have to be submitted by the grower to an official body for a seal of approval. For example new regulations issued in 1974 by the French Government introduced analysis *and tasting* for all *appellation contrôlée* wines. *

☐ In the cellars of the *négociant* or shipper, the selected wine may be nursed a little further up to the stage of shipment in cask or bottling. During this period, it is tasted by professional buyers with a keen eye on price, style and potential development.

☐ Competitive tastings at wine fairs and conventions. These are fairly

*The main provisions of the new Decree 74-871, which will have a five-year introductory period before full implementation, are as follows:
ARTICLE 1: the wines for which an AOC is claimed cannot be put into circulation without a 'certificate of agreement' issued by the *Institut National des Appellations d'Origine des Vins et Eaux-de-Vie* (INAO) after an examination conforming to the terms of Article II of EEC regulation No. 817/70 of the Council of 28 April 1970.
ARTICLE 2: the examination, organised by INAO or local wine-growing *syndicats* consists of an analysis and tasting, the latter carried out by a special Commission, along officially laid-down fixed lines of procedure.

common in wine-producing countries, particularly in California, Australia and in Eastern Europe.

☐ After shipment in cask* it will rest in the cellar of the shipper or merchant until it is ready for bottling. The firm's tasters – and the analyst, if there is a laboratory – will examine its condition prior to bottling. Thereafter, from time to time, 'quality-control' personnel will keep an eye on the behaviour and development of the wine in bottle.

☐ The next category of tasting is the trade tasting, where the merchant, wholesaler or institutional buyer selects wine for re-sale. This sort of function may be of the headline-hitting variety in a vast candle-lit cellar, or may take the form of a quiet, down-to-earth tasting in a some-what clinical-looking tasting room. In either case, the buyer is on the lookout for wines either to lay down or to offer for laying down or, of course, for immediate consumption.

☐ Lastly, the keen amateur, with a good cellar, will taste his own wines to see how they are progressing and to choose wines suitable for a particular occasion, guest or type of food. He also will taste them, before serving, to make sure that the condition and temperature are right.

Tasting contexts

In all the above instances, it will be seen that each taster will be examining a wine in a different context and with a particular point of view: the wine-maker with a paternal eye, the buyer with price and market uppermost, the quality-control taster or chemist for condition and stability, the salesman for attractive qualities of price and style, and the final consumer with his palate, pocket and future entertaining plans in mind.

From the second stage to the penultimate, the value of the tasting to the participants will increase roughly proportionately to the range of wines on show. Even at a dinner party, the qualities of a really fine wine will be more fully revealed if paired off with, or preceded by, a lesser but comparable wine.

It follows, however, that as each category of taster is apt to concern himself with a limited aspect of wines, his general perspective will narrow, and it is only too easy for the professional *and* the amateur to adopt, out of habit, a 'blinkered', one-sided approach. The professional, with limited time at his disposal and a narrow objective, cannot be expected to probe and analyse the hidden depths of sixty young wines at 10 o'clock in the morning. Nevertheless, he should be conscious of the dangers of slipping into a rut. Equally, the amateur will enrich his experience by taking more than a superficial glimpse at the wonderful liquids that nature, with man's aid, has contrived for his pleasure.

---

*To the United Kingdom or elsewhere in Europe. Importation in cask is not permitted in the U.S.A.

III: When to taste: some basic points

The only way to appreciate wine is when a few men, who understand and enjoy it meet together, feeling free to luxuriate in the delight imparted. ...
T. G. SHAW Wine, the Vine and the Cellar, 1863

Morning freshness

The best time for doing anything constructive and creative is when the mental and physical states are freshest. This, for most people (whether they appreciate it or not) is in the morning. It is said, incidentally, that the palate is sharpened by hungry anticipation, which would indicate the benefits of pre-luncheon tasting sessions.

In point of fact, the majority of trade tastings *are* held in the morning. The most quiet and business-like tastings may be held around 10 o'clock, possibly at noon. Tastings to which trade or private customers are invited usually begin about 11.30 and may end with a buffet or light luncheon, during the course of which selected wines are shown off against appropriate food. (It is not without significance that the simpler and more wholesome the repast, the better the wines show; there are fewer distractions of flavour. For example simple cold roast beef and mild English cheeses provide the most perfect foil for good French reds.)

Evening sessions

Early evening tastings are also popular. They are generally held by the trade between 6 and 8 o'clock to attract customers who would otherwise find it difficult to attend during their working day. These evening tastings tend to be less serious – people are tired after a day's work and feel more in need of a reviver than the concentration needed to taste in earnest. Or they have had time to go home and change, and may treat the whole affair as a rather jolly social occasion. The wine merchant host dispensing his stock-in-trade may not really mind, so long as the party-goer leaves in a sober enough state to remember the name of his firm!

Amateur wine society tastings are also held mainly in the early evening, for similar reasons, though the degree of serious attention is often more marked.

General points to observe

Before getting down to the serious business of tasting, there are quite a number of general points to watch out for. Not all are appropriate for professionals and amateurs alike. Some are quite basic, some merely minor details and some may even appear trivial. Not necessarily in order of importance, they are as follows:

No smoking

Smoking in a tasting room is not only considered ill-mannered and offensive, it will seriously reduce the effectiveness of other tasters, particularly if they are non-smokers. It is difficult enough as it is to detect subtleties of bouquet without a smoke-screen attacking one's nostrils at the same time.

It should be said immediately that the rule of 'no smoking' in the tasting room does not mean that a taster should not smoke at all. In point of fact, there seems little evidence that a smoker's tasting abilities are less than a non-smoker's. The palate appears to compensate for this regular coating of tobacco smoke and nicotine, and there are numerous examples in the trade of fairly heavy smokers being good tasters. Some are even reputed to have a 'drag' at a strong French cigarette between tasting sessions.

Make notes

Remembering the taste of a wine, but forgetting its name, and vice versa, is very tiresome. It is astonishing how easy it is to forget the name of even an outstanding wine only an hour or so after tasting. These blank spots occur to the professionals, whose memory is cluttered with multitudinous examples, as well as to the tyro. It is particularly frustrating for a merchant to recommend a range of wines to a customer and for the latter to note one in particular that he thought outstanding – only to forget its name.

The answer is, make a note. At least scribble on a piece of paper the name of the wine and vintage, and whether it was agreeable or not.

Note-making can turn into a fetish; it can become a hobby like collecting stamps. The moderate use of sensible notes will, however, be invaluable and even a good memory will be better served by the briefest record of name, description and opinion. Various methods of note-making are dealt with in Chapter XI.

Good company

An exchange of views helps to shape and confirm a hazy impression, revealing aspects of a wine that might not otherwise have been noticed. It goes without saying that the company in question must be equally interested – a large party of uninterested observers or hard drinkers is merely off-putting.

An organized tasting group is likely to be the best solution, not the least of its virtues being the increased purchasing power of pooled resources which make it possible to accumulate a wider range of better-class wines.

Quite the best advice one can give the newcomer is to taste in the company of an expert, or at least with a taster of some experience.

The only snag about a free-for-all tasting is the distraction of chatterboxes. It is difficult enough as it is without being interrupted between sniffing and note making.

Related wines

It is perfectly possible to judge a fine wine on its own, but its true qualities will be thrown into much sharper perspective when it is tasted alongside another wine, even if dissimilar in style. By far the most revealing type of tasting is one where comparisons can be made between wines of the same vintage but from different districts, or from the same vineyard but of different vintages.

Appropriate order of tasting

Dry before sweet; young before old; modest before fine. Whether red wines are tasted before white depends on the relative 'weights'. Light dry whites are better before fuller-bodied reds, but light young red wine is probably better tasted before full-bodied sweet white wine with heavy 'extract' and residual sugar.

It is perfectly possible for a professional taster to assess the relative qualities of a large range of related wines, say thirty to sixty. It is doubtful, however, whether more than an essential facet or two can be obtained by tasting on this scale, and certainly for the beginner, six to ten wines are usually as many as he can effectively cope with. Over this number the taste buds can become tired, the mind confused.

Try to relate the time spent per wine on the total available or on those you wish to taste. Nothing is more frustrating than to find that you have spent nearly all the tasting session on a handful of wines at the beginning, invariably the least interesting, leaving yourself neither time nor energy for the best at the end.

Temperature and presentation

Present the wines appropriately: red wines at room temperature, white wines (rosé, champagne, sherry) at cellar temperature (see page 20). Do not open too far in advance: up to one hour before the tasting is a reasonable average. Decant old and mature wines, as the sediment is likely to well up in the bottle unless extremely gently poured.

Taste 'blind'

'A sight of the label is worth fifty years' experience' – a cynical truism: for what an impressionable lot we are! Even the most sternly disciplined taster is biased by the merest glimpse of the label, even by the shape of the bottle. One can also be swayed by the appreciative – or otherwise – noises and looks of other tasters.

For a completely objective assessment, arrange the wines to be tasted in numbered glasses (use a wax pencil or self-adhesive labels on the upper side of the base), the numbers being related to the bottles which are, of course, out of sight. Alternatively, cover up the bottles, standing the glasses in front. Failing this, turn the bottles round so that the labels cannot be seen.

Don't drink, spit

It is nothing short of ridiculous to *drink* one's way through a tasting. How can the last few wines yield more than a hazy impression? This is particularly important when tasting fortified wines.

To taste critically is one thing, to enjoy wines with a meal is another. So when tasting, spit out the wine, don't swallow it. The performance is not considered rude, nor need it be undignified; it is a perfectly sensible convention.

In a *chai* or cellar it is considered perfectly normal to spit on the floor, which anyway is often of earth, or, if of concrete, strewn with sand or sawdust. All proper tasting rooms are furnished with sink spittoons, usually with running water. If a tasting is held in a public building, or in a private room, spittoons should be provided. A wooden wine case containing sawdust is simple to prepare and has the advantage of dimensions generous enough to accommodate all but the very worst shots. It is best not to spit on the carpet!

Taste the best

Ordinary wines are for drinking, not tasting. Modest-to-medium quality wines afford good practice and can be interesting, but they are often indefinable and rarely clear-cut in character. The true characteristics of a district or a vintage are best exemplified by wines of high quality. In any case, an assessment of lesser wines must inevitably be made in relation to an exemplar or touchstone. Don't be an inverted snob; occasionally buy a great wine and try to see what extra it has to offer.

Physical hazards

Don't waste time trying to taste if you have a streaming cold. Catarrh doesn't help either. Clear your nostrils.

Don't try to taste with traces of alien matter in the mouth. Alkaline toothpaste interacts with the acidity of wine. Fruit, with its high acid content, will affect the taste too; so will highly-spiced breakfast sausages, and so on. Fish and crabmeat stuck in the teeth can be a hazard.

Order and discipline

Taste in a regular sequence; examine the appearance of the wine first, its bouquet next and finally its taste. And within those three main sub-divisions, look out for definite salient features.

A prepared tasting sheet or book can be a great help in this respect, and guards against the temptation to leapfrog from glass to glass in a haphazard fashion.

This does not mean, in fact, that one should never dodge back and forth. Indeed, when tasting wines in ascending order of quality or descending order of age, the earlier wines can be seen in sharper perspective if one re-tastes them after completing the range.

Awareness of context

This is highly important and usually under-rated. There are several relevant aspects.

The climate as well as the food has to be considered. For example, a charming light wine with a highly refreshing acidity drunk with fresh trout on the banks of the Loire in midsummer, or a *vinho verde* enjoyed with rich pork in the Minho can taste entirely different on a cold and misty autumn evening with Arbroath 'smokies' in Scotland. Quite apart from the need to match wine with food, the temperature, humidity and time of year have a bearing. The colder the climate, the more full-bodied the wine needs to be.

It is no coincidence that port was created by the English (and Scots) in Portugal for their compatriots at home; they were aware that high spirit and sugar content would warm the cockles of their kinsmen's hearts. Nor is it a commercial fluke that cream sherry and brown sherry (now a bit old-fashioned) sell particularly well in the north of England. Vintage port is at home in chill university Senior Common Rooms, burgundy with barons of beef in draughty guild halls, and so on.

Wine and food

The inter-relationship of wine and food is too well known to be re-stated here. Certainly, endless books deal with the subject. Suffice it to say that a good wine can be wasted in a wrong food context. It may seem unenterprising, but it is usually safer and more sensible to follow the conventional rules.

What is less well appreciated is that those who are used to tasting mainly fortified wines (sherry; port in particular), may find some difficulty in adjusting their palates to very light table wines. Also, those who are

fortunate enough to afford, and to restrict their interest to only the finest
wines, will tend to undervalue the quality of much lesser wines. The
opposite does not, however, obtain. A regular drinker of ordinary table
wine does not tend to overvalue a fine wine when it is put before him;
if anything, he is more likely to be unappreciative of its subtleties and to
wonder why anyone could be crazy enough to pay, for one bottle,
a sum that might cover his daily fare for a week.

IV: The senses of sight, smell and taste

I am tempted to believe that smell and taste are in fact but a single composite sense, whose laboratory is the mouth and its chimney the nose.
BRILLAT-SAVARIN, The Physiology of Taste

The senses

Those fortunate to have eyesight employ this sense every minute of their waking day. Our eyes have plenty of practice. Even colour awareness, for example, which may not be fully developed as an artist's, is normally at a high level, mainly because of constant usage. The enormous advantage that colour has over smell and taste, is that it can be so much more easily described and conveyed from one person to another.* In the last resort it can be accurately reproduced.

On the other hand, the senses of smell and taste are rarely so highly or so continuously employed. Indeed, the level of awareness can be abysmally low. This is partly owing to the fact that the sense of smell is easily fatigued (even after a short time a worker in a chocolate factory or a tannery does not notice the smell) and partly because it is less frequently exercised.

Flavour is a compound of taste and smell, yet although the sensitivity and selectivity of the latter sense is infinitely higher than that of taste, it is the least consciously applied.

In relation to wine, most people 'taste' – in a superficially literal sense – but very few deliberately and consciously smell the wine first, let alone derive any positive information or pleasure from that act. What is far too little known is that a great deal of what one wants, or needs, to know about wine can be detected from its appearance and bouquet alone. The actual taste on the palate basically confirms the impressions that sight and smell have previously conveyed and of course adds to the sum total.

Sense of smell

Smell is the oldest and most primitive of all the senses; more than any other it invokes memory in a particularly direct manner. The 'smell-brain,' with its direct contact with the memory areas, can act as an immediate catalyst of recognition and identification that accounts for the value and importance of the 'first impression' that, justifiably, can be relied upon by experienced tasters.

Let us deal now in some detail with the mechanics of smell. Physically, this is what happens: the stimulus that excites the sense of smell results from certain substances, in solution, coming into contact with myriads of highly complex cells in the nose. Such substances usually enter the nose

---

*A complete and universally accepted scientific analysis, classification and description of smells and tastes, despite a mass of multi-disciplinary research and enquiries, appears to defy solution. Perhaps, slightly out of context, I can quote the last sentence of the epilogue of Dr. Harper's *Odour Description and Odour Classification*: 'Perhaps at present this remains more of an art than a science'.

in the form of vapour. In the case of wine they are conveyed by volatile esters and aldehydes. At this stage they are taken over by the olfactory system. The first pair of cranial nerves are called olfactory nerves. They begin as specialized olfactory cells in the lining of the upper part of the nose. Fibrils from these cells pass up into the olfactory bulbs, lying in the base of the skull. From the bulbs the olfactory tracts – thick bands of white brain matter – pass backwards to enter the brain, and the fibres contained in the tracts are brought into relationship with nerve cells in certain parts of the brain. The original stimulus at the nerve endings is, in effect, converted into a sensation for the brain to interpret.

An interesting fact is that over-prolonged exposure to one smell may reduce the effectiveness of that smell, but that other smells may be readily detected. From a practical point of view this means that it is pointless to sniff too long or too frequently at one wine. If the first impression is lost, it is probably better to move on to the next wine. Then move back to the original or tackle it again after a rest (see also Chapter V, page 19).

In my experience, passing one's nose over the glass and lightly inhaling will often yield virtually all the wine has to offer. It is sensible to swirl the wine gently and smell again more carefully, but rarely, I find, is it really necessary or beneficial to sniff vigorously and inhale deeply (as advocated by the distinguished authors of two recently-published French text books) except, perhaps, to isolate a fault in a poor wine.

Chambré-ing red wines and cupping the glass in one's hand both have a good practical reason. There is evidence that whatever the state of the substance having smell, its appreciation depends on that substance passing into the solution with which the olfactory cells are normally bathed. But the higher the molecular weight of the wine, the greater the need to encourage the process of vaporization. This is accomplished by gently raising its temperature. A 'cold start' accounts for the 'dumbness' of a massively constituted red wine, even if mature. It also accounts for the remarkable after-taste and 'lingering farewell' that arises from the naso-pharynx as the mouth-warmed wine passes down the throat and the released volatile ethers rise through the back nasal passages.

Conversely, light wines, with low extract and 'weight' do not need to be warmed. Those which are light but relatively high-toned (such as a Moselle of a moderate year) will release bouquet with an impact that is immediate but which lacks depth. They rely not on an aftertaste but on a high degree of natural acidity to give the wine a 'finish' – to which chilling adds crispness.

Some pungent substances have a more physical impact, stimulating the nerve endings in a tactile sense. For example, sulphur dioxide can be detected by a prickle in the nose even though its presence in the wine may not be strong enough to affect the olfactory system. Certain of the higher alcohols can also have a similar effect, producing a feeling rather than a smell. Acetic acid can be both felt and smelled.

Sense of taste

Next, let us examine the physical nature of taste. The sense of taste depends on the stimulation of organs known as taste buds. These are mainly situated in the tongue, though a few are found in the soft palate, and their sensitivity varies. The nerves connected with the taste buds carry impulses to the nerve centre in the medulla (which is the name for the marrow at the top of the spinal cord), whence they are carried to the parts of the brain towards the tip and inner sides of the temporal lobe—in close relation to the area of the brain concerned with the sense of smell.

To cause the necessary stimulus, a substance must be in solution and the sensation it evokes relates to one, or a combination, of the four so-called primary* elements of taste: sweetness (best appreciated at the tip of the tongue), sourness† (upper edges of the tongue), bitterness (at the back of the tongue), and saltiness (at the sides).

If one has this basic understanding of which parts of the palate detect which common tastes, it will be quite apparent that to 'peck' at wine, i.e. to take a very small sip or leave only the tip of the tongue in contact, will not enable the taster to appreciate more than a fraction of the wine's physical characteristics. A reasonable mouthful must be taken and it must be swirled round the mouth so that all the taste buds can get to work on it. Some experienced tasters take a large mouthful and draw air across their palate, sometimes with rather an offputting guzzling noise. This has the effect of spreading the wine across the whole of the palate and allowing the volatile scents to ascend the back of the nose for the olfactory nerves to play their part.

Sense of touch

Tactile impressions, implying the use of fingers and hands, do not, strictly speaking, apply to the tasting process. Nevertheless, wine produces reactions which have certainly nothing to do with sight, smell or taste, and are as equally certainly tactile. For example, the body, 'weight', of the wine in the mouth, the evaluations of certain extracts which are detected physically in the mouth, and carbon dioxide in *spritzig*, lightly sparkling or fully sparkling state.

Also certain chemical reactions in the mouth and nose affect the tactile sense more than the sense of smell. Sulphur dioxide, already mentioned, is an example.

Sense of hearing

The sense of hearing does not seriously enter into wine tasting. There is nothing in wine like the delightful crunchiness of a crisp biscuit – unless it be the anticipatory pop of a cork, the sound of pouring and tinkling of glasses, the fizz of champagne or the ministering sizzle of Alka-Seltzer the following morning! As for those audible signs of approval, considered good manners at the Chinese dinner table, they are far too delicate a subject for western eyes (and ears).

Gastric stimulation

Before leaving the physical element of wine tasting, it is perhaps worth mentioning an important by-product; in some instances this might be considered the be-all-and-end-all of wine drinking, viz. the stimulation of the gastric juices. Quite apart from its health-giving natural properties,

*"There is relatively little evidence to support the concept of primary tastes' – Dr. Roland Harper *The Human Senses in Action* – see Appendix **V**.

†Sourness, in a wine context, has a denigratory connotation. Acidity, an essential component, is the word tasters use (see glossary).

[16]

wine is a superlative aid to digestion. The appetite is whetted by the smell of a refreshingly youthful white wine, and by the tingling dryness, the acidity and even the slight bitterness of many reds. The nerves of taste and smell are stimulated which, in turn, increase the activity of the salivary glands. Also, through a reflex nervous action, the wine markedly increases the amount of digestive juice secreted in the walls of the stomach; it flows more rapidly, and the movements of the stomach are speeded up. This stimulation of the muscular wall of the stomach extends to that of the bowel, greatly aiding the digestion of the accompanying food.

But let us turn to the act of tasting . . . . .

Shape and dimensions of the ISO tasting glass*

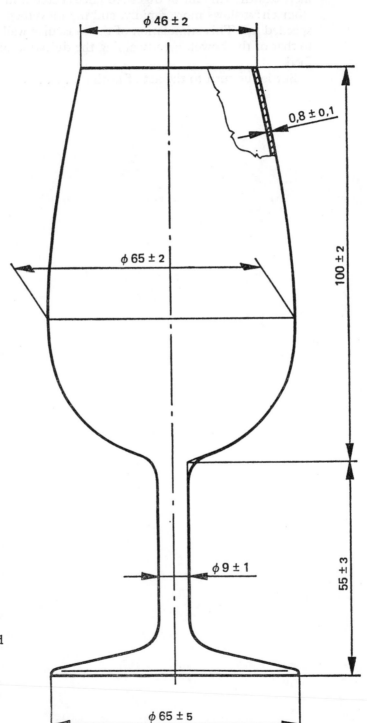

Dimensions in millimeters

Overall height:
155 ± 5 mm

Total capacity:
215 ± 10 ml

Tasting quantity:
50 ml

Manufacture:
colourless
transparent crystal
glass containing
about 9% lead.

φ 46 ± 2

0,8 ± 0,1

φ 65 ± 2

100 ± 2

φ 9 ± 1

55 ± 3

φ 65 ± 5

*This is an extract from International Standard ISO 3591-1977 reproduced with permission of ISO. The complete standard can be obtained from ISO and its member bodies (in the United Kingdom, the British Standards Institution).

V: How to taste

Your true amateur sips his wine; as he lingers over each separate mouthful, he obtains from each the sum total of pleasure which he would have experienced had he emptied his glass at a single draught. BRILLAT-SAVARIN

Tasting sequence

The order in which one tastes a wine is based on the natural physical movement of the glass from table to mouth. First of all, the glass is picked up and the wine examined. This is stage one. As it is raised towards the mouth the nose sniffs the bouquet – stage two. Then the lips meet the rim of the glass, and stage three, the literal tasting, commences.

But, over and above this, there is a correlation: what one sees is 'taken up' by the nose; what one tastes tends to confirm visual and nasal impressions. The logical conclusion is a stage four, the summary of overall impressions, and the final verdict.

Before starting, make sure that the glasses are suitable and the lighting adequate.

Glasses

If you do not possess an ideal* tasting glass just use a conventional, tulip-shaped, crystal-clear wine glass, *not* a fancy or coloured one.

If tasting a range of wines, use matching glasses of a generous size. Pour an equal measure in each so that the relative depth of hue can be seen at a glance. Do not fill the glass more than half full, as it will be easier to tilt above a white table top, an essential manoeuvre if the informative colour at the rim of the wine is to be seen clearly. It will also enable the wine to be swirled around in the glass without spilling, collecting the volatile substances prior to nosing.

Pick up the glass by its stem or foot, not by the bowl. This makes it easier to examine the wine, particularly if held in front of a lighted candle. It also avoids the influence of body warmth and has the minor virtue of avoiding finger marks on the sides of the glass. (Handling old bottles can be a dirty business; wine itself tends to be sticky if dripping or spilt).

Lighting

Daylight is best, preferably a good *north* light, as artificial lighting can affect both hue and tone. In particular, avoid fluorescent lighting; it makes red wine look unhealthily brown, even blue-tinged. Candle light is glamorous; it enhances the appearance of both wine and the lady guest! But for a serious tasting the only benefit of a candle is to reveal the true degree of clarity of the wine. For this reason, it is useful in a cellar when young wine is drawn from the cask, or when decanting a bottle before dinner.

*An ideal tasting glass is illustrated opposite. There are several acceptable variations on this theme.

Temperature

Make sure the temperature of the wine is correct: room temperature for reds (including port), cool for rosé (say 50° to 55°F or 13° to 14°C) and cold for white (around 48° to 50°F or say from 11° to 13°C). The actual room temperature will naturally vary from place to place and with the time of year – but will be a pleasant *natural* temperature. The range could well be anywhere between 60° and 65°F, 16° to 18°C. Incidentally, make sure the glasses for red wine are at the same temperature and not brought out of a cold cupboard at the last minute.

Stage I: Appearance

Colour or hue

Under the heading of appearance,★ the taster looks at three facets: colour, depth and clarity. Each of these facets will be examined in turn.

Most table wines fall in to one of three basic categories: red, white or rosé. Fortified wines vary: sherry is technically a white wine and ranges from pale straw-yellow to deep brown; port may be red or white, the former ranging from deep purple, ruby to pale tawny.

Perhaps the most important thing to bear in mind is that the colour should be appropriate for the type and age of wine.

RED WINES

What we know as a *red* wine will, in fact, vary in hue from deep purple through various shades of red to mahogany or even amber, depending mainly on its state of maturity, the vintage and the district. The length of fermentation, the time the must is kept on the skins, have a major influence, so does the time kept in cask. (The red colour comes from a group of pigments called anthocyanols extracted from the grape skins by the action of alcohol. The ageing process has a direct effect on colour, the red pigment being precipitated by tannin during the period of maturation both in cask and bottle.)

Purple

Indicates extreme youth or immaturity. Almost all red wine in cask will have this colour. The time taken in bottle to lose its strong purple tinge depends on the initial depth of colour.

Ruby

Self-descriptive. The colour of a young port or a fullish claret or burgundy, having lost its pristine flush of purple.

Red

In vinous terms red is the colour approximating to 'claret'. It indicates the transitional period between youth and the acquisition of maturity and bottle age. Garnet is the desirable hue of a fine Italian wine.

Red-brown

In a table wine this hue indicates maturity (for example, claret with five or more years in bottle, burgundy three years or more – depending on the quality of the vintage). A brown tinge can also result from baked vines after a hot summer, also from artificially heated and 'cooked' wine (i.e. during fermentation), or from aeration and oxidation owing to over-exposure to air in cask.

Mahogany

A more mellow, subtle red-brown indicating considerable maturity

★I use the term in its broadest, and generally accepted sense: that which is perceived by the eye, and not in a limited sense like 'clarity'.

	(a claret with ten to twenty years' bottle-age, burgundy of a moderate vintage with over ten years' bottle-age).
Tawny	A term, like ruby, usually associated with port. It describes a hue that has been attained through loss of colour over a period of years in cask, a natural but expensive maturing process. Cheaper commercial 'tawnies' are made by blending white wines with red.
Amber-brown	Indicates either a wine of very considerable age or one which is prematurely old and/or oxidised. Once the healthy ruddy glow disappears, the wine is usually dead.

WHITE WINES

All white wines contain some degree of yellow pigment (of the flavanol group) but in some the concentration is low. They will vary, therefore, from virtual colourlessness through the palest yellow/green and deeper shades of yellow, to gold and to deep amber-brown.

Dry white wines usually start off life pale in colour, and, unlike red wines, gain colour with age.

Sweet wines generally start off a fuller shade of yellow, turn to gold and then take on an amber-brown tinge with age (see also 'depth', overleaf).

Young natural sherry is basically a pale straw-yellow, the deeper shades being the result of ageing and/or blending. Practically all the dark oloroso and brown sherries gain their colour from added *color* wine of one sort or another.

Pale yellow-green	A distinct green tinge is quite common in youthful white wines, due to residual chlorophyll, and is a particular, if not essential, characteristic of a Chablis or a young Moselle. It is rarely seen in the white wines grown in hot climates.
Straw-yellow	A pleasant lively colour common to the majority of white wines, particularly the drier ones. In Burgundy, Meursaults tend to be more yellow than the Montrachets, and in Alsace, *traminers* more yellow than *rieslings*, though this cannot be relied on.
Yellow-gold	Not an abnormal colour for a dry white wine but most frequently seen in the sweeter varieties such as Sauternes and high quality German dessert wines of beerenauslese and trockenbeerenauslese quality.
Gold	Generally indicates either a lusciously sweet wine, or one with considerable bottle-age (for example, a white burgundy, usually pale straw when young, will develop a slight golden sheen after about six years in bottle).
Yellow-brown or old gold	The colour of many dessert wines, fortified ones in particular. However, a brown or orange tinge in a white table wine indicates considerable bottle-age, over-maturity or even oxidation. Many white burgundies will take on an unhealthy brown tinge after about twelve years in bottle; yet a fine Sauternes may not develop it for thirty years or more.
Maderised	This word is used to describe the appearance and condition of over-maturity and some degree of oxidation. A maderised white wine presents a dull appearance, with a pallid yellow-brown colour.

Brown	Probably well past drinking (unless of course, it is a sherry of that name or the ruddy tawny-brown of an old port).

ROSE WINES

Wines described as rosé can vary considerably in colour and depth. Each district has its own style, depending on the type of grape used and on the method of making. The better rosés are made from black grapes, the skins being left in contact with the fermenting must just long enough for red pigment to be extracted. Cheap rosés are sometimes a blend of red and white wines.

The colour of a rosé is half its charm. A rosé wine is usually drunk young, for if allowed to age it would lose its freshness of colour and taste. Some rosés begin life the colour of onion skin, a characteristic of those wines appropriately termed *pélure d'oignon* and *vin gris*.

Rosé	The perfect rosé should not look like a watered-down red wine, nor should it support an excess of orange or purple. It should be positive, clear and appealing.
Orange	Some grape varieties produce a distinct orange tint, some don't. Pure orange is not a desirable hue although a pleasant orange-pink is quite normal and characteristic of many rosés from the Loire. Orange is even more marked in Provence and the hot south.
Pink	A self-descriptive hue, often suggestive of artificiality. Any suspicion of a blue tinge indicates unhealthiness, probably from bad fining or metallic contamination.
Depth of colour	Although the basic fullness or paleness of any wine will depend to a certain extent on its origin, the relative depth of colour will give a good indication of its physical content.

RED WINES

Depth, in association with the actual colour or hue, will also give a clear indication of the age and maturity of the wine. For example, a very full, nearly opaque, red/purple wine will almost certainly have more than its fair share of tannin and other natural component parts. A colour like this will only be seen in a well-made wine of a fine vintage, its properties being derived from rich, fully-ripe grapes with sun-thickened skins. The converse applies equally: a pale red wine results from too high a yield per hectare, from hasty vinification, or a poor year in which the grapes have failed to mature and whose skins are thin and deficient in pigment.

WHITE WINES

Dry	In regard to young dry white wines, depth of colour is relatively unimportant. The variations are comparatively small and the connotations usually inconclusive. A *very* pale Moselle, for example, is likely to be neither better nor worse than one which is medium-pale. White wines tend to deepen with bottle-age.
Sweet	The depth of colour of sweet white wines is more meaningful. Care must be taken not to confuse the deep gold of an old Sauternes of

a great vintage with 'maderisation'. Château d'Yquem of the 1921 and 1929 vintages is very deep – deep gold, not deep brown – indicative of the extraordinarily high initial sugar content and extract. The point is that these vintages were deep in colour when young. Beware also of drawing a wrong conclusion from a *pale* old Sauternes. This is indicative of either a lighter vintage and/or over-sulphuring prior to bottling. The latter acts as a preservative, inhibiting development and colour change.

It is sometimes difficult to judge the comparative depth of colour of two matching wines. One method is to fill each of the glasses to the same height, place them side by side and look at each from a position vertically above; another method is to arrange a light behind the glasses and compare the relative depth of colour of the shadow cast by each wine on a white table top, a little–known but very effective way for all colours of wine.

Clarity

This is of prime importance in the various stages of development of all wines from the time of fermentation, during life in cask, through to the time of bottling. Thereafter, white wines should be star-bright and trouble-free. Only red wines are normally expected to throw a sediment in bottle.

Fine wines often have extra lustre and luminosity.

Tastevins

The rather attractive silver *tastevins* which are sold in Burgundian souvenir shops (and used as ashtrays) are, in fact, traditional tasting vessels with a peculiar usefulness. The circular indentations in the shallow sides reflect candle light across the metal base to reveal at a glance in an ill-lit cellar the clarity of the new wine drawn from the cask. A *tastevin* is also more convenient to carry around and less fragile than a glass though it is pretentious to take one to a normal tasting; a proper tasting glass is more useful. (In the Burgundy and Beaujolais regions the *tastevin* also has symbolic guild connotations).

Upper surface

The upper surface of the wine in the glass is worth inspection. It should of course be bright. If it appears dull, iridescent or bitty, trouble may be indicated. With very old wine, I also look out for the tell-tale bead of persistent small bubbles around the meniscus which generally gives advance warning that the wine is cracking up.

Cloudiness

Hold up the glass to the light, or against a candle. A dull cloudiness or obstinate haze of suspended matter in bottled wine is a bad sign; in normal circumstances, the wine should be returned to the supplier. Incidentally, think carefully before condemning a cloudy *red* wine. Was it recently delivered or carried up from the cellars hastily and clumsily? Old vintage port usually has a heavy sediment or 'crust' and even when carefully decanted may still have 'fliers' or 'beeswing' (very descriptive) in it. The latter are normal (and tasteless) and should be ignored.

Cork, not 'corked'

Tiny pieces of floating cork are harmless; so are most forms of sediment which settle easily in the bottle. Bits of cork in the wine may be owing to a bad corking machine or, more usually, to the careless use of a cork-screw. Wine with cork floating on it is *not* 'corked' – an ignorant mis-understanding in restaurants that too often leads to completely fatuous and unnecessary complaints. Just pick the cork out!

Crystals   Flakes of tartaric acid crystals are sometimes seen in fortified wine and white table wine. They are usually caused by a sudden change of temperature. These generally settle quickly, are quite harmless and do not impair the flavour.

Limpidity   Lastly, it is an appropriate phenomenon that a really beautiful limpid colour is often indicative of a great or fine wine whereas an ordinary blended wine will often have a dull nondescript lack-lustre appearance.

Grades of clarity shade down from brilliant, star-bright, bright, clear to dull, bitty, hazy and cloudy.

Legs

I have never been a 'leg' man myself; indeed, there seems to be some confusion over the term in relation to wine.

Full-bodied wines, those with high extract and with considerable glycerol content in particular, form 'legs' – globules with extended tails – which fall slowly to the surface of the wine *after* the glass has been swirled. This can, with some justification, be considered to presage richness, but I personally prefer to rely on my palate. First of all, glycerine can be added to wine (mainly to soften over-acidity; surprisingly, it does not add much to the viscosity) and carelessly washed and dried glasses can play havoc with the meniscus.

As far as I can see, 'legs' have nothing to do with any 'surface-tension pump' which is supposed to draw a film of liquid up the sides of the glass.

Level or ullage (in bottle)

Although this relates to the appearance of wine in the bottle rather than in the glass, it is probably appropriate to refer to it here. A lower level than normal can be due to:

Short fill   The result of sloppy bottling and careless inspection; level low neck or around upper shoulder. Fairly rare and usually little to worry about.

Reduction   A natural contraction★ which can occur in bottle, over a period of time. In my experience mature burgundies can show a $1\frac{3}{4}$ in. to $2\frac{3}{4}$ in. ullage without deleterious effect.†

Cork failure   The commonest cause of ullage is cork failure due to cork weevil or lack of springiness due to old age. Cork weevil is not uncommon, particularly in carelessly-maintained private cellars. It is about the only thing which will affect the condition of old vintage port, particularly if the protective wax seal has broken or worn away: the weevil will bore holes in the cork and let air in. The wine will become acetic, or at least be tainted with the soiled cork.

Corks, like human bodies, eventually lose their suppleness and springiness with age. After twenty years or so, the elasticity of cork weakens, though high-quality long claret corks can protect wine for a century. Uneven ullages, quite common with very old wine, say pre-world war two, are almost always due to cork failure. Re-corking – standard practice in the great *châteaux* and *domaine* cellars – is the answer. Failing this (as with the great Rosebery pre-phylloxera clarets) regular

---

★I gather that if a gallon of water and a gallon of alcohol are mixed, the total measures less than two gallons.

†I frequently come across ullaged bottles in old cellars. If the ullages, in a bin-full of one wine, are fairly uniform, and the corks and caps appear sound, I do not worry overmuch.

[24]

waxing of seals and capsules, whilst otherwise remaining unmoved in a cold slightly damp cellar, will preserve the corks, and wine.

Ullaged bottles *can* turn out surprisingly well. Sometimes the air in the space does not harm the wine. If the cork is not foul, and the colour of the wine deep and good, the wine, even though old and vulnerable, may miraculously survive. But it must be of high quality to begin with. *Old champagne* Old champagne can *look* ullaged, but if the cork and foil are sound this ullage generally turns out to be carbon-dioxide out of solution. No longer bubbly, the champagne will have turned into a calm, golden-sheened wine much beloved of English connoisseurs, somewhat to the exasperation of the French.

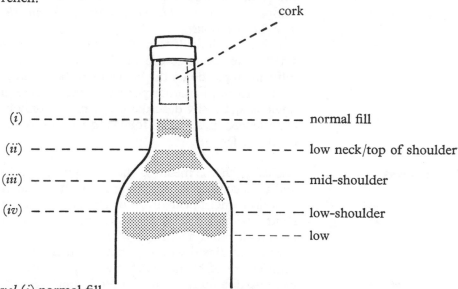

level (i) normal fill.

level (ii) acceptable level for Bordeaux over 15 years old. If a young wine, possibly natural reduction, *or* short fill. Highly acceptable – 'good level for age' – for any pre-1930 wine.

level (iii) if under 25 years old, possible cork failure. Not abnormal, certainly acceptable, for *very* old wine, though there is always an element of risk.

level (iv) almost certainly indication of cork failure. Oxidation/acetification risks high, whatever the age.

Below *level (iv)* the wine will almost certainly be undrinkable, and unacceptable for sale except, if rare, as a curiosity.

Stage II: Nose or bouquet

The importance and value of nosing a wine are generally underrated, for a great deal of valuable information about any wine may be gained from the smell alone. The first impression is generally the most telling.

The best procedure is to take hold of the stem of the glass lightly and, keeping its base on the table, rotate it briskly. This exposes the maximum surface area of wine, encouraging the release by vaporization of its ethers. It also neutralises the smell of a dirty glass.

Deep breathing exercises do not help; on the contrary, they tend to deaden the senses. In my experience one does not need to sniff hard to detect the bouquet in the upper nasal passages, though a long gentle inhalation often reveals more facets, as does rousing the wine by shaking it vigorously in the glass (see also pages 14 and 15). I believe it was the late Allan Sichel who recommended 'short sharp sniffs with the mouth open,' though I cannot say this works with me.

The smell of wine can be of two types: that which reminds one of another smell, or one that is, with experience, recognizable as a more-or-less pure chemical substance or compound. In essence however, the wine taster has to learn to detect and recognise different grape aromas, youthfulness and maturity, pure wine scents and, with more experience, complex overtones. *The more mature the wine the more important the nose factor becomes.*

It is most difficult to analyse and describe most common-or-garden smells; even more so the subtleties of a refined bouquet. And if it is difficult to pin down the elements of bouquet, it is almost impossible to convey them to another person. Some of the following characteristics are obvious and easily describable, some can only be recognized by an experienced 'nose'. The following facets should be examined, preferably in this order:

Cleanliness

Basically what is meant is that the wine should smell like wine, pure and unencumbered. Anything redolent of bad cabbages, old socks, vinegar, almond kernels, pear drops or any clearly extraneous or foreign smells, should be regarded as suspect, to say the least. In practice this is an automatic reflex action.

Sulphur dioxide, quite common on European white wines – it is reminiscent of burnt match sticks or the whiff of a coke oven – is regarded as more of a nuisance than an 'off' smell. Aeration, decanting, swirling in the glass, lessen the effect.

If no off-odours are readily apparent one passes on to the more positive wine smells.

Grape variety

The experienced taster will next look out for the first major clue to the origin of the wine: the characteristic grape aroma.* The classic 'noble' vines, *cabernet-sauvignon, pinot, riesling, traminer*, and so on, produce their own individual aromas. However even these are not always easy to detect, and the only way to memorise them is to taste and retaste first-rate examples until their characteristics are firmly lodged in the mind (see pages 31 to 38 and appendix i).

Minor wines: those made from lesser grape varieties and those from minor districts will less frequently produce a distinct and recognizable aroma. More often it will be just vaguely 'varietal', and if totally indistinguishable but pleasant will merely be described as 'vinous'.

Youth, age and maturity

The age of a wine can be accurately judged on the nose by an experienced taster. It is not as difficult as it might appear at first, and, as always, the

---

*The expressions aroma and bouquet are used here in the senses defined in the glossary, Appendix i. However both are frequently muddled in usage – by me as well as others.

comparison of good specimens of different vintages is the best way to learn.

The physical components of young wine tend to be pronounced and raw as they have had little time to settle down and blend together. Youthful acidity has a mouth-watering effect. A raw cooking-apple smell indicates excess malic acid and is frequently found in young, unripe white wines, particularly from poorer vintage years.

As the wine mellows with age, its bouquet* becomes noticeably softer and more harmonious. It develops what is known as 'bottle-age'. It is almost impossible to describe bottle-age; on most white wines this shows up as a definable 'honeyed' quality; red wines become richer and deeper with bottle-age. Complex and mellow are perhaps the operative words. A wine with too much bottle-age will show deterioration by taking on a flat, dull, toffee-like smell (maderised) or what is known as bottle-stink (oxidation, which can produce a smell like bad cabbages). The point is that bottle-age is part and parcel of the maturing process, the softening up, the harmonising, that is revealed to the enquiring taster.

Fruit

'Fruit' is a desirable quality, but it should be noted that a wine can be described as fruity without having any trace of grapeyness. A distinctly grapey bouquet is only found in wines made from certain unmistakable grape varieties (see pages 36 and 37, also Appendix i).

Depth and intensity

A bouquet can be described as light or deep, intense, nondescript, superficial, full or rounded, depending on the development of the wine. However, care must be taken not to be misled by the 'full' i.e. fully-developed bouquet of a ripe but poor quality wine, or, conversely, by the 'dumb' or undeveloped bouquet of a very fine but immature wine.

It is hard to define quality. What one is looking for is an unfolding, an exposure, of bouquet that is rich, many-faceted, but soft; forthcoming yet harmonious. And the bouquet of a *great* wine is not only over-whelmingly beautiful but tends to linger in the glass even when it has been drained to the last drop.

There are many conventional terms used to describe the bouquet of wine and the principal ones are defined in Appendix i.

Stage III: Taste

The taste, or gustatory stage, should first and foremost confirm conclusions drawn from the appearance and bouquet. The palate is a fairly basic evaluator. In fact it provides the taster with rather less information than the eye and nose, though unless it is new in cask, the younger the wine the more important the palate element becomes. This is not to suggest that taste is unimportant. Far from it. In any case a factor, excess acidity for example, not spotted by the nose may be detected on the palate: a sort of long-stop situation.

*The expressions aroma and bouquet are used here in the senses defined in the glossary, Appendix i. However both are frequently muddled in usage – by me as well as others.

As indicated in Chapter IV, there are several points of oral contact which will reveal different taste characteristics – the tip of the tongue (sweetness), the upper edges (acidity), sides (saltiness) and back of the tongue (bitterness). For this reason, one tiny sip is usually inadequate. Do not peck at the wine; take a reasonable mouthful, swirl it round the mouth; then spit it out and repeat the process if necessary.

It is recommended that the elemental characteristics that are detected on the palate be noted in strict order. It matters less what the order is than that the order is a habitual one. In this way one avoids overlooking vital factors. Here are the basic 'movements' and observations. Read through and then refer to the glossary, Appendix i.

Dryness and sweetness

A basic and easily-judged constituent, particularly important in white wines. Do not be misled by thinness or excessive acidity, which tend to make one underestimate the actual sugar content, and vice versa. There is also an apparent sweetness, due to ripeness, noticeable in hot-country wines.

Acidity

Acidity is a major element in the make-up of any wine. It gives a wine purpose, life, 'zing' and finish. Extremes of acidity are, however, undesirable. Excess sugar and glycerol, natural or otherwise, tends to mask the true degree of acidity.

Body

The 'weight' of wine in the mouth basically is the result of its extract and alcoholic content. An important factor that varies according to the district, vintage, vinification, etc.

Tannin

Although disagreeable on the palate (harsh, dry and mouth-puckering) it is an essential element of any young *red* wine. Tannin precipitates proteins and acts as a general preservative. It is essential for long life.

Tactile stimuli

Smooth, creamy, velvety qualities can be felt in the mouth; so can astringent factors, and the burning sensation of alcohol.

Flavour

This is all-important. Even if it is impossible to describe, at least record whether agreeable. The word 'typical' should be used sparingly. The intensity and length of flavour reflect quality.

Balance

This is basically what the wine maker, the merchant and the connoisseur seek. What is meant by balance is that all the component parts are in harmony, with, for example, no excess of acid or tannin, at the time when the wine should be ripe for drinking. The whole point is that individually the component parts are useless, indeed mainly unpleasant to the taster; it is in combination that they make wine, and, when complete and in perfect balance, *fine* wine. Two things have to be borne in mind: one is that the intrinsic components will vary from district to district, from style to style; and that over a period of time the balance will almost certainly change.

Take a red Bordeaux: when young, its tannin and acidity will be exposed and raw. It takes time, say 5 to 10 years, for the component parts of a fine wine to 'simmer down' and marry, becoming a well-knit harmonious drink. (It is the job of the merchant to be able to judge the future development of what seems to the layman a raw young claret.)

In the case of a fine German wine, the grower strives to achieve, almost from the start, the right balance of acidity, sugar content and alcohol so that it can be early-bottled to capture, for his particular market, the desirable fruity-acidity which, with aroma and bouquet, happen to be the touchstone of fine Hocks and Moselles.

Finish

A clean, crisp finish is the mark of a good, well-made wine. Poor quality wines finish 'short' or tail off to a watery, insubstantial end. Top quality wines have long finish, often extending to an aftertaste or lingering 'farewell'.

Quality, finesse, elegance, breed

The elements of quality are represented by the completeness and balance of component parts. Quality can be assessed by the length of time the flavour lingers in the mouth, by its richness and subtlety and by its aftertaste. A variety of expressive abstract terms can be used to express degrees of quality. They tend to be subjective and should be chosen with care. See Chapter XII and Appendix i.

Stage IV: Conclusions

It is hardly surprising that there should be a relationship between the appearance, bouquet and taste of any one wine. Yet, in my experience, most tasters tend to examine each stage or facet in isolation whereas some, myself included, see each stage as a revelation leading naturally to the next, and irrevocably to a logical conclusion.

The context is important. One makes allowances for minor wines and is hyper-critical of fine wines, just as one should be tolerant of the weaknesses of the ill-educated or the less fortunate and perhaps more critical of the well-endowed and beautiful people! If my friend Edmund Penning-Rowsell seems at times over-critical it is because he is bringing to bear his highly-tuned faculties on wine of high calibre or pretensions. In another context, the speedy visit to a dim cellar or a casual dinner party are hardly the places for a prolonged and detailed critique.

Again, in practice, the experienced taster need not tabulate precisely, in thoughts or words, his reactions to appearance, bouquet and taste; indeed, with our wonderful built-in computers, a look, a sniff and a mouthful can – if correctly programmed – give us instant summaries equivalent to 'a magnificent, soft, supple wine of great breed, intensity; fully mature' or 'raw, harsh, immature and poor quality – discard'.

But for the student, for the beginner or for the conscientious connoisseur, a tabulated tasting note arriving at a considered conclusion is a useful exercise. It gathers the thoughts and ties up the loose ends.

The conclusion therefore should summarise compactly the salient points and add comments regarding the overall quality of the wine, its maturity, possibly its value and certainly its rating in the context of the particular tasting.

If you happen to be a judge in a competition, then almost certainly your notes and conclusions will have to be made in a precise form, usually tabulated with numerical values. Scoring is dealt with briefly on page 85, but for exhaustive details I must refer readers to Amerine or Vedel (see bibliography, Appendix v).

Lastly, I would again draw your attention to the chapter on the use of words and the glossary of tasting terms (appendix i). These not only give you a very wide range of commonly, and less frequently, used terms, but the definitions – which admittedly are on occasion subject to slightly different interpretations – strive to give readers not only a clear indication of their meaning but, in the case of terms like tannin, explain something of the physical or chemical background.

Price

Although not a 'tasting' quality, price is a factor that cannot often be ignored. It is certainly the common denominator of all wine trade tastings except those concerned solely with the wine's physical development or condition.

Only a real wine snob or hypocrite (often the same person) and perhaps the carelessly rich, need not heed the price factor, though this does not mean that 'pure' or abstract tastings, comparing one wine with another, are not desirable and valuable. But for most purchasers and consumers of wine, price *is* the final arbiter, in the sense that value for money is sought and appreciated, as much as, if not more than, pure quality.

Recent years witnessed an escalation of fine wine prices that appeared to be out of all proportion. In fact, we had a simple supply-and-demand situation – surging world demand for wines in geographically limited supply. Rising costs, inflation and devaluations have added their toll. Unhappily the speculator added pressure to the naturally increasing demands of opulent civilizations nurturing more and more wine enthusiasts. There was one consolation: the previously often impoverished wine grower at last received a return on his capital, using his new found wealth to replant derelict vineyards, replace old vines and renew his equipment.

Increased production, the flight of the speculator – dumping stocks en route – and a recession have all combined to reverse the market situation. The price of wine is at last returning to levels which make sense to the drinker but which are temporarily, one hopes, painful to the producer and trade. What is really needed is balance: an appreciative consumer who will pay a respectable merchant or restaurateur a reasonable price, which in turn allows the vineyard owner and wine-maker a fair return for his labours, the risks and vicissitudes.

It should be remembered however that, historically, the finest wines have never been cheap. They were originally the sole province of the aristocratic, wealthy and privileged classes, and I dare say that quite a few didn't really appreciate them to the full – then as now!

At least, by increasing our awareness and appreciation we will not waste the opportunities of tasting fine and rare wines when, as they surely will, they present themselves for our delectation.

VI: Origin of taste characteristics

O for a draught of vintage! that hath been
Cool'd a long age in the deep-delvèd earth. KEATS

I now propose to deal briefly, and necessarily inadequately, for it is a huge subject, with those factors at the growth and production end which create and influence the taste of wine.

It could be argued that this should have been dealt with first. However, tasting is primarily an end-product exercise, and it is the art of tasting and not vine growing and wine making which is the least documented of all wine knowledge and, after all, the subject of this book.

Background knowledge

We should, however, concern ourselves with grape varieties, with soil, climate, methods of cultivation and wine making, if only for one reason: the knowledge of the effects they all have on colour, bouquet and flavour. All this is not, however, necessary for the simple appreciation and enjoyment of wine, so don't please think that you *have* to read about, let alone master, this subject in order to be numbered amongst the world's happy band of wine lovers.

But if you *do* want to learn more, where do you begin? What has the greatest bearing on the style and flavour of wine? The variety of grape. Is this constant? No, it depends on the soil upon which it is grown. Is this combination constant? Again, no; the latitude, climate, the care of the vine and length of fermentation and, of course, the level of skill at every turn; all these have a bearing.

However, before going into more detail it is important to realize that although it is convenient to break these elements down and study them separately, they can never, in practice, be completely isolated. They interact to create the final end-product.

Grape varieties

Grape varieties are all-important. They have to suit the soil, the climate and the economy of the region. Most good wine primers name and describe the main species and varieties, some also deal with vine diseases and pests, grafting and so on; just a few relate all these to the end-taste. What I propose to do here is to list the main varieties, starting off with the four most 'noble' grapes, giving examples of the wine they make, followed by the rest in alphabetical order.

First of all, it is important to remember that the bulk of the world's wines are of ordinary quality, made from vines comparatively easy to grow and prolific yielders. Different grapes are blended; final wines may be blended. The resulting appearance, smell and taste are usually unremarkable and un-noteworthy.

The great wines of the world, i.e. those with exceptionally marked taste characteristics and quality, are made from a limited range of 'noble' grape varieties, produced mainly on difficult, sometimes almost barren, soils and terrains, in delicately uncertain, not to say risky, climates.

Indeed, I would go as far as to say that today the only wines really worthy of the interest of the true 'amateur' and connoisseur are those made by scarcely more than a handful of grape varieties. Familiarize yourself with these; they give the highest satisfaction to the senses, and their characteristics, once mastered, can be more easily memorized than those of lesser varieties. The latter may well be interesting and pleasant, but the fact is that they rarely merit a second glance. Their role is to provide an agreeable accompaniment to a well-cooked meal.

Age of vine

A highly important factor and one often overlooked is the age of the vine. It is commonly known that a newly planted vine does not bear wine-making fruit for three years. Thereafter the quality of the wine increases steadily with age as the roots grow deeper down through soil and subsoil; then for a period the vine combines high quality and substantial yield. Finally the plant hardens and tires, and its production often falls to uneconomic levels.

Here are the four leading 'noble' grape varieties, followed by other well-known, and lesser known, varieties in alphabetical order:

Cabernet-Sauvignon

Without hesitation, I put *cabernet-sauvignon* at the head of the great red wine grapes of the world, not because I am dogmatic enough to place the finest claret, which it produces, above the finest burgundy, but because it maintains a recognizable style and character even when transplanted out of its classic home region, Bordeaux. For example, a well made 'cabernet' from Chile, Australia or California will have a basic family resemblance despite overtones produced by differences of soil and climate.

The *cabernet-sauvignon* gives claret its quality; its depth and richness of colour, aroma and wealth of bouquet; the firm, hard, keeping qualities and length of flavour. The three keys to its recognition are the deep colour, the characteristic grape smell of fresh blackcurrants or cedar, and particular flavour in combination with tannin and acidity. These may all vary somewhat in strength, not only because of differences of soil and microclimate within the Bordeaux area, but because the *cabernet-sauvignon* is rarely used alone but grown alongside and combined with other claret grapes, mainly *cabernet-franc* (like the *sauvignon* but slightly less distinctive) and *merlot* (softer and fatter in character).

I think it is useful practice to familiarize oneself with the *cabernet-sauvignon* characteristics at their most pronounced. If you are well off, try Château Mouton-Rothschild. It has an opacity of colour, opulence of bouquet and concentration of flavour that make it almost a caricature of a great claret. If your finances don't permit you to run to a first growth try, for grape character, Malescot-Margaux or Lynch-Bages of a good year. Memorize the grape aroma in particular.

Riesling

German wine lovers may place the *riesling* first, but I place it second in the hierarchy of noble grape varieties. It is certainly the most versatile and ubiquitous white grape, being grown in several European wine districts as well as in almost every major region in other continents. Like the *cabernet*, it has enormous strength of character which shows through even after transplanting.

It scales the greatest heights in Germany, in the Rheingau and Moselle districts in particular, but can often be seen at its most recognizably straight-forward in Alsace.

The *riesling* makes a wine with a colour ranging from very pale straw with a hint of green, through pale yellow to deep gold (the latter would be a rich dessert wine, particularly with bottle-age). Its bouquet will be fruity but not grapey, forthcoming, refreshing and clean as a whistle; sometimes flowery, honeyed, and, when made from fully ripe grapes, almost muscat-scented. Most *rieslings* are dry to medium-dry but – another proof of its versatility – it can make the richest and sweetest dessert wines of the world. Another marked feature is a firmness, almost steeliness, of body, and fresh, crisp fruit acidity. It is never very high in alcohol but has an excellent balance and finish.

If I were to suggest a copybook specimen I would choose a *Riesling Réserve Spéciale* or *Exceptionnel* bottled by one of the better Alsace growers and shippers, like Hugel or Trimbach. They are remarkably pure wines and very good value.

If you want to take a more opulent hock as an example, I would choose a *riesling spätlese* or *auslese* of the 1971 vintage from one of the several distinguished Rheingau growers such as von Simmern, Graf Eltz, Dr. Weil, Matuschka-Greiffenclau, etc. These wines are not cheap but, bearing in mind the present price of other top-class wines – champagne, claret and burgundy, for example – they are much less extravagant than you might think.

Pinot

I place the *pinot* second amongst the red grapes of the world, for though (at its best) in Burgundy it produces wines of sublime richness and quality, it does not seem to make wine of so marked and recognizable a character when grown in other districts, whether elsewhere in Europe or in other continents. Perhaps I should mention here that it is also (with its white counterpart) *the* grape of Champagne.

A ripe *pinot*, vinified in a traditional way, from a good 'climat' in the Côte de Nuits will have a velvety depth of colour (true 'burgundy red') with pronounced viscosity ('legs'). Its bouquet will be sweeter and more opulent than its counterpart in Bordeaux; and it will have a consistency on the palate that is both full and soft, alcoholic and velvety. The first main recognition signal is in the nose, in particular the *pinot* grape aroma which I, personally, find impossible to describe (though the head of a school of wine suggests boiled beetroot as a memory trigger). The *pinot* smell must be identified, isolated and memorized. It is only from *ripe* grapes that the true *pinot* aroma emanates.

The next key factor is the weight of the wine, allied to softness. There is much less of the searingly mouth-drying tannin of its great rival, produced by the *cabernet*, in Bordeaux – a characteristic which makes a *pinot* much 'easier' to drink and to sell.

It is the hardest thing in the world to recommend perfect examples in the modest to middle-priced ranges; perhaps a bit easier in the pricier realms. To discover the flavour and character of a good *pinot* from the Côte de Nuits buy a fine vintage wine bottled by a leading grower or Domaine such as de Vogüé, Daü or Damoy; or a good Côte de Beaune, from the Domaine Louis Latour or Drouhin; the higher-priced wines of shippers like Jadot or Faivelet; or La Tâche of a great year.

Chardonnay

This is the white version of the *pinot* and makes the great white burgundies of the Côte de Beaune and Chablis (not to forget Champagne). It is also responsible for perhaps the finest varietal wines made in California.

It thrives on chalky soil and it produces a wine varying in colour from very pale straw to a fairly pronounced straw-yellow (a feature of many Meursaults). A good specimen will have a fresh, crisp, sometimes smoky, fruity (but not grapey) bouquet – very hard to describe. It will be dry; from the firm steely dryness of Chablis, and to some extent of the Puligny-Montrachet, to the softer dryness of Meursault, and the nutty dryness of Corton-Charlemagne. It will have a fair amount of acidity and body, and a subtlety and austerity of flavour that understandably, but paradoxically, attracts claret lovers.

High quality white burgundies have a rich yet understated flavour; poor ones can be thin and dull. Louis Latour makes consistently fine Corton-Charlemagne, as does the Domaine Leflaive good steely Puligny-Montrachet. In California, growers like Dr. David Bruce and Chalone produce stylish examples; in Australia, Tyrrell and Lake.

Other grape varieties in alphabetical order

Aligoté

White grape producing minor white wines in Burgundy. Pale; pleasant but undistinguished aroma; dry, light, pleasant acidity.

Blanc-Fumé

See *Sauvignon-blanc*.

Bual

White grape making one of the richer madeiras.

Cabernet-franc

One of the main Bordeaux varieties. A close relation to the *cabernet-sauvignon*, fairly similar in style. Known as *bouchet* in St.-Emilion.

Carignan

Prolific and rather neutral red wine grape (France, N. Africa and elsewhere).

Chasselas

Another rather neutral and prolific vine. White.

Chenin-blanc

A major variety making the dry-to-medium-sweet white wines of the mid-Loire. A pleasant waxy aroma, plenty of refreshing acidity. Also grown in California, Australia and South Africa (known as *Steen*).

Fendant	The same as *chasselas*. Grown in Switzerland.
Folle Blanche	White and ordinary.
Fürmint	Hungarian white grape producing one of Europe's least-known great classic wines: Tokay. Straw-coloured wines, with a distinctive old-apple-like aroma when young, richly honeyed when aged. Ranging from dry to sweet, concentrated essence.
Gamay	This is not a noble grape, but in one region, Beaujolais, it excels and produces a wine of such distinct character that it ranks only just below *pinot* in flavour.
	The *gamay* mainly produces a light red wine; often lightish pink-purple in colour and certainly light in alcohol and extract. Its most marked characteristics are a charmingly forthcoming and fruity bouquet, unique in character – difficult to describe but fairly easy to recognize. Lightweight and fresh in the mouth, with little tannin but quite a lot of acidity.
	Grocers' beaujolais won't do. If you want a fair specimen, choose an unblended single-vineyard wine. Such wines are still not expensive, and most enlightened merchants stock one or two.
Gewürztraminer	In some ways, the most disregarded of the noble grapes. Yet it has an immediately attractive and recognizable style, easy, perhaps too easy, to appreciate and drink; for its opulent flavour tends to overplay its hand and then begins to pall; a white wine, at its best in south Germany (the Palatinate particularly) and Alsace.
	In colour sometimes deeper and more yellow than the *riesling*, its most noticeable feature is a scented aroma, reminiscent of lychees, herb-like and spicy (*gewürz*). It ranges from fairly dry to medium-dry; has an equally flowery flavour but is soft and almost velvety, lacking the tinglingly refreshing acidity of the *riesling*.
	Once again, for a pure specimen try an estate-bottled Alsace version, of a recent good vintage. The old classic *traminers* of the Palatinate have never been very popular outside Germany and are even losing favour there, being rather earthy, heavyweight, and sometimes clumsy in style. They can, of course, be magnificent. Better to take the advice of a specialist Rhine-wine shipper if you want to taste a good specimen.
Grenache	Fruity, pleasant red wines: lightish in colour but not in alcohol; agreeable lightly-fruity aroma. Grown in the southern Rhône, the Midi, California, and Australia.
Gros Plant	A synonym for Folle Blanche, making a useful, rather neutral dry wine in the lower Loire.
Grüner Veltliner	Milk-soft, dry white wine from Austria.

Malmsey	White grape grown in Madeira making a deep amber-brown sweet dessert wine with characteristic 'warm' tangy bouquet.
Merlot	A major variety grown in Bordeaux, giving claret flesh and roundness, complementing *cabernet-sauvignon;* dominant in Pomerol, St.-Emilion.
Müller-Thurgau	A now well-established *riesling-sylvaner* cross producing a pale coloured, grapey scented white wine of easy and attractive character in most German wine districts, particularly in Rheinhessia. Also grown successfully in England.
Muscadelle	A familiar sounding grape name. One might expect it to be raisiny in smell and flavour, and it is. Usually of very pronounced character, it is used to add particular savour, in sparing quantities, to sweet white Bordeaux.
Muscadet	Name of grape and type of white: pale, bone-dry white wine from the lower Loire.
Muscat	Rich, amber-coloured fortified dessert wine, with rich, tangy aroma and madeira-like acidity. Grown in several parts of the world but reaching its summit in north-east Victoria (Australia).
Muscat (d'Alsace)	This is a somewhat unusual relation of *muscatelle*. It looks like any dry white wine, smells overpoweringly grapey and sweet, but is usually bone-dry on the palate. The best (Hugel again produces fine specimens) seem to combine the grapiness and richness of a *traminer* with the dryness and crispness of a *riesling*.
Nebbiolo	One of the great red grapes of Italy, making the deep, powerful firm and classic Barolo – try one of Marcarini's or Prunotto's; also Barbaresco.
Palomino	*The* sherry grape: pale, dry, refined. With *flor* culture develops characteristic bouquet, unmistakable but difficult to define.
Pedro Ximenez	Classic sherry grape used for blending. In Victorian times drunk as a dessert wine: brown, almost opaque; rich, burnt, tangy nose; excessively sweet, rich and heavy.
Petit Verdot	Often used as the fourth component, albeit in a small proportion, of claret. Slow ripener. Tends to be 'green' and tart in lesser years.
Pinotage	A red grape, a cross between *pinot* and *hermitage*, grown in South Africa, producing a rather jammy, clumsy, alcoholic wine.
Pinot blanc	Once confused with *pinot chardonnay* but although of similar style, less distinguished.
Pinot gris	Rather four-square, somewhat undistinguished, white wine.

Rülander	Synonym for *pinot gris* making a pleasant, slightly innocuous white wine in the Rhinelands of Germany. Pale coloured, grass-like aroma, mild.
Sangiovese	One of the noble grapes of Italy, the principal variety making Chianti. Firm, full, long lasting and with a distinctive dry, almost bitter finish. Try the Nozzole, or an old Frescobaldi wine.
Sauvignon blanc	A curiously attractive variety; in bouquet and flavour something of a cross between *cabernet-sauvignon* and *traminer*. In other words, it combines a spicy, blackcurrant aroma, with a mouthwateringly refreshing acidity. Rather fashionable, but can be thin if poor. It is grown under this name in Bordeaux, and is one of the components of Barsac and Sauternes, adding the necessary crispness and acidity. Of the same grape family but called *blanc fumé* it is responsible for the wonderfully crisp, dry, fruity wines grown at Pouilly-sur-Loire and for the wines of similar style at nearby Sancerre.
Scheurebe	A successful crossing used in Germany, particularly in Rheinhessia and the Palatinate, producing a dramatically grapey aroma and rather facile flavour to match. Lacks the firmness and balance of the *riesling*.
Sémillon	A white grape, one of the major components of Sauternes and Graves. It has quality and style, a soft 'lanolin' nose, but somehow lacks fruity acidity, which is why it is usually vinified alongside the *sauvignon blanc*.
Sercial	Originally the *riesling*, making the palest and driest madeira.
Shiraz	A red variety extremely at home in Australia and South Africa, making deep-coloured, swiftly maturing yet long-lasting, soft but alcoholic wines reminiscent of the Rhône, with an unmistakeable and, at first, strange, tangy aroma aptly described as 'sweaty saddle'.
Siegerrebe	Another somewhat exotic, grapey-smelling white wine grown in Germany.
Steen	A long-planted variety, similar to, probably identical with, the *Chenin-Blanc*. Grown in the Cape vineyards of South Africa and certainly making the best and most characteristic dry white Cape wines.
Sylvaner	Though making a familiar Alsatian wine type, *sylvaner* is not a 'noble' grape. It is a more humble but nevertheless distinct variety. It would be both unkind and misleading to describe it as 'the poor man's *reisling*', but it makes a useful dry hock-style wine of less marked character. The *sylvaner* is also grown in Germany, producing a second-rank wine, lacking the finesse and crispness of the *riesling*, except in Franconia where it produces great Steinwein.
Syrah	A fine variety grown in the Rhône valley, responsible for red Hermitage: deep, firm long-lasting wines (Paul Jaboulet makes wonderful examples). Also used in Châteauneuf-du-Pape.

Tokay Synonym for the *pinot gris* grown in Alsace. A firm white wine with few marked characteristics. Do not confuse with Hungarian Tokay.

Traminer See *Gewürztraminer*.

Trebbiano A major Italian white wine grape used in Soave, Orvieto, Chianti and elsewhere, the style depending on the vinification but mainly straw-yellow in colour, with a waxy, rather unfruity, nose; dry, four-square and rather unexciting flavour and finish.

Viognier An unusual grape which in Condrieu, at Château Grillet, in the Rhône makes white wine of considerable style and distinction.

Zinfandel A grape peculiar, and well-suited, to California making red wines of considerable distinction, many with considerable staying power.

Soil

The taster can comfort himself in the knowledge that convention – historical trial and error – and more recent research work have pretty firmly established exactly what variety of vine flourishes in which type of soil. It is of interest for us to note that the best wines are made from vines grown in uncompromising terrain; often upon ground too poor to support any other crop: schistous rock (port), gravel (claret), slate (Moselle), large pebbles (Châteauneuf-du-Pape), and so on.

It seems that soil plays a major but subdued supporting role, at best when unobtrusive, supplying *just* those minerals, storing moisture and so forth, to allow the vine to struggle for existence but no more. Certainly good fertile soil encourages the vine to become over prolific, producing quantity at the expense of quality. Over-use of fertilizers has a similar effect and, in addition, gives undesirable off-tastes to the vine.

Fine *white* wines, requiring freshness and acidity, thrive on chalk. Fino sherry, for example, and champagne. In Burgundy, along the Côte de Beaune, the natural adaptation of vines to soils can be seen dramatically by walking from the red wine *climats* of Corton round to the chalky slope of Corton-Charlemagne, where only white grapes are grown.

Some wines – red Graves, some Rhône wines, Palatinate hocks – smell and taste 'earthy'. Some, as in parts of St.-Emilion, reflect the high iron content of the soil by having an iron taste (if you've ever had an iron tonic or some of the more medicinally reminiscent Australian 'burgundies', you will recognize this feature). The Napa valley soil gives its wines a distinct and recognizable volcanic richness and earthiness.

Sub-soil The importance of the sub-soil cannot be overstressed. Much of the richness and extract of a fine wine is drawn from the right sort of sub-soil by the deeply thrusting roots of the mature vine.

There are often subtle and complex differences between two red wines made in the same way, from the same grapes, but from neighbouring vineyards. These differences of flavour and bouquet are mainly owing to the make-up of soil and subsoil (almost certainly more important) and the balance of minerals. The drainage and the aspect also play a part, mainly in the retention of heat and moisture.

Rarely, however, are the effects of soil on taste *direct*, and when they are these tend to be in the nature of 'overtones' of bouquet and taste, which makes their origin the more difficult to pin down. I readily admit to being ill-equipped to delve deeply into these fascinating sub-strata of soil and mineral tastes. At least the taster should be *aware* of their presence and indubitable influence, and should try to recognise those soil characteristics that *are* pronounced.

Climate

After the indefinable complexities of soils, the effects of climatic variations are more frequently documented and more easily understood. Like soil, though, climate influences the taste of wine through its effect on the grape. Understand the reaction of the grape to sun, cold and rain, and it is easier to recognize the end product of a given vintage.

Geographical

Geographical influences – the limits of latitude, proximity of rivers and bodies of water, height above sea level, and so on – can take a back seat, from the taster's point of view. The wines we normally come across will not be grown in unsuitable areas. This is not *our* problem. Climatic variations, however, are of considerable interest and significance.

Climate

There are three broad aspects of climate in so far as they affect wine:

Zones

The first concerns the consideration and comparison of the effects of two quite different climes: the gentle but significant variations in a temperate zone (the northern half of Europe, for example) and the less variable, hotter and drier, zones exemplified by North Africa, the uplands of South Africa, the irrigated areas of South Australia, and southern California. The *comparative* uniformity and reliability of the latter areas make life less hazardous for the grower but somewhat less interesting for the discerning drinker, as the wine is of a more even quality, with fewer surprises, and rarely, if ever, scales the heights. The motto of fine wine could well be *nil sine labore*, for it is the struggle against the elements that kindles quality.

Annual differences

The second aspect of climate is confined to the temperate zones. It consists of the *annual* variation and is of enormous importance to the entire concept of vintage wines. This aspect will be dealt with in some detail below.

Micro-climate

The third aspect is the micro-climate: the variations due to the lie of the land – sun traps, the susceptibility to pockets of frost and fog, etc. – which occur within wine areas and from vineyard to vineyard.

The connoisseur will mainly be concerned with 'aspect two', vintage variations, but in the process of describing the general effects of too much sun and too much rain, the implications will throw light on the extremes of 'aspect one': that is to say, the character of wines made at the outside edges of the permissible vine-growing latitudes will reflect the characteristics outlined in the following paragraph.

Variations

Too much sun and too little rain (in a given year or in a particular part of the world) will reduce the quantity of juice in the grape and thicken the skins, thus producing excess colouring matter and tannin. In some northern zones, at the end of the ripening period the skins may shrivel and crack, letting in undesirable ferments. The first fermentation may be hard to control, risking spoilage. (Choice of grape, soil, irrigation and vat cooling systems are counter factors in hot dry areas.) As a result, the wines, if red, will be full of colour, alcohol and tannin, heavy, coarse and hard. If white they will lack acidity and, in consequence, be heavy, flat, flabby, charmless, and with little bouquet.

Too much rain and insufficient sun will increase the volume of juice. However, the grapes won't ripen fully, so the sugar content will be low, and the wrong sort of acidity high. This will result in a low alcoholic content and pale colour (if red). The wine will be thin and tart, unbalanced and short-lived. If steps are taken during vinification to increase the sugar content artificially, and to stabilize the wine, it can be made into a tolerable beverage but will never be fine.

Vintage charts

Those much maligned aids, vintage charts, do at least provide a handy *aide-mémoire*, for their ratings, in effect, summarize quite accurately the overall weather conditions which have affected a particular area in a given year. For example, the year 1963 rates 'one' (out of seven) under the 'Claret' heading of the current Wine & Food Society Vintage Chart. This low rating is a fair reflection of the poor weather conditions prevailing that year in Bordeaux, resulting in equally poor wine. However the north of Portugal enjoyed an excellent combination of sun and rainfall in 1963. Under the heading 'Port' it justly rates seven out of seven.

It is with vintages like 1964 that generalizations become dangerous. Heavy rain-storms in the middle of the vintage were disastrous for those Bordeaux growers who were holding on for further ripening. The early, pre-rain pickers like Château Latour were fortunate. The late pickers, including Lafite, Mouton-Rothschild, Calon-Ségur and Lynch-Bages, made comparatively puny, wishy-washy wines. Over the river, in St.-Emilion, the rain was not as severe as in the Médoc and the wines were uniformly more successful. Charts *can* be useful, but watch out for the exceptions. Better a generalisation than no information at all.

My tip for beginners is not to be bamboozled and bedazzled by airy-fairy vintage talk. Forget the bottle and label for a minute and remember that the precious liquid inside stems from a *crop* affected by weather conditions like any other crop. It would all come more naturally, for the English at any rate, if we were all to realize that on the occasions when *we* have enjoyed an unusually stunning summer the odds are that the rest of northern Europe has too, and that the vintage will probably be good.

Wine making

Whereas the care of the vine – the annual toil in the vineyards – can vary in degree and attention from grower to grower, we can reasonably assume a tolerable standard, to enable the owner to earn a living. His husbandry will affect quality and quantity; the over-use of certain fertilizers may also affect the taste, but it is when we come to wine *making* that the skills and particular techniques of the owner, grower or cellar-master will have the most direct bearing on the colour, bouquet and flavour of the wine which he brings into the world.

Improvements

Thanks to the activity of schools of oenology and viticulture, to governmental and local institutes and advisory bodies, much less bad wine is made these days. It is however totally untrue for them to claim that without their help and advice no good wine would be made. Great wines were made before oenology, as an exact science, was conceived; just as wine was sold before 'marketing concepts' were invented. The sciences and pseudo-sciences are servants and modern aides; rarely the originators, never the masters.

In the more ignorant and uncontrolled days of the past, galloping fermentation by wild yeasts would frequently give an off-taste to the wine, over-hot fermentation might breed microbes in the absence of SO_2 and the heat would usually 'cook' the wines; sulphur would be over-used, and so on. All these errors and omissions would spoil the smell and taste in some detectable way.

Nowadays, so far as red wines are concerned, the principal worry is that the demands of commerce – wines for quick maturing and quick turnover – are being met by speedier fermentation and increased blending. The former leads to paler-coloured red wines with less tannin and extract, the latter to neutralization of character and quality (see Chapter II).

Care

Care of the wine prior to bottling – or the lack of it – can have a direct effect on taste. For example, the woodiness which comes from wines being kept too long in new casks, or too long in cask at all; the acrid effect of over sulphuring; the sour overtones of a wine left on the lees too long, and the vinegary smell of a 'pricked,' probably neglected, wine.

The effect of age

It is a useful over-simplification to say that 'wine is a living thing'. It implies, quite correctly, that wine, once made, is in a constant state of change and development, first in cask, then in bottle. Again, for simplicity, I am ignoring the use and effects of glass-lined vats, ionization, pasteurization, refrigeration and all the sophisticated 'tools' and techniques employed these days by large undertakings to keep their wines stable and as unchanging as possible. My terms of reference in this final section are limited to the ageing, maturation, of *quality* vintage wines, insofar as they affect taste.

| **Quality and maturity** | Perhaps I should define 'quality vintage wine' or *vin de garde*. It is a wine of one good vineyard* of one vintage whose raw young component parts are present in strength and balance, so that over a period of years, first in cask, but mainly in bottle, these parts will 'marry', settle and soften into one harmonious but characterful whole. |

Red wines

Young red wine will start life with a full colour, plenty of tannin, acidity and alcohol. Over a period of time, depending on the strength and degree of these basic elements, the colouring matter will be precipitated by the tannin (see 'colour', page 20), which itself gradually loses its harsh dryness. The acidity will tone down, and the whole ensemble will look more mellow, smell sweeter and richer, with subtler overtones and scents, and the effect in the mouth will also be soft, mellow and harmonious – no discordant edges – with layers of flavour and a long finish and fragrant aftertaste.

Red wines repay keeping best. But do *all* red wines repay keeping? The answer is no. Cheap branded wines, non-vintage blended wines, and very minor clarets and burgundies will probably improve with just three months' to a year's bottle-age in your own cellar (do not rely on the merchant to give an ordinary wine bottle-age, he will endeavour to sell it soon after bottling). Even well-made but minor *bourgeois* wines, claret in particular, are not worth holding over-long. It is important to keep things in perspective and realize that a 20-year-old *bourgeois* claret will not have improved to 'classed-growth' quality simply by keeping. It may have mellowed nicely, but in the final analysis it will only taste like a minor claret, just older, tireder and possibly sadder!

White wines

It is commonly accepted that *dry* white wines are not meant to be kept, but to be drunk whilst young and fresh. What is little known is that the really good dry whites, particularly from classic districts, not only keep well but will develop with bottle-age quite distinctive qualities of colour, bouquet and flavour. For example, a 1952 Montrachet, a 1949 Corton-Charlemagne, a 1947 Vouvray, many 1953 Rhine wines of quality, from a good cold cellar, can still be on the 'plateau of perfection' now, in the mid-1970s. In financial terms, unlike their red equivalents, they may not have appreciated proportionately in value; but in sensory terms they can be a revelation. Which really is what tasting is all about. . . .

Elders and betters?

Summing up, don't expect age to confer upon an ordinary or middle-class wine qualities it never had to begin with. The only wines that will keep and blossom in interest and character over the years are the 'pedigree' wines: first-growth claret and some of the other classified growths, single-vineyard burgundies bottled at the *domaine*, and the rare aristocratic Chiantis and Barolos; the great dessert wines like vintage port, a rich tokay aszu, the great Sauternes, sweet Loire wines (particularly Coteaux-du-Layon), and Rhine and Moselle wines of *auslese* and *beerenauslese* and *trockenbeerenauslese* quality.

---

*A particular *marque* of vintage port may stem from one or more vineyards, but will be made under the control of a single shipper.

VII: Main regional characteristics

Name Sirs the wine that most invites your taste. JOHN GAY,
Poem on Wine, 1708

Introduction

This chapter is an attempt to bridge the gap between tasting techniques and specific types of wine, to give the reader some indication of what to look for when faced with a wine from a major region or district or type.

Method

Rather than give a 'blow by blow' description of each wine, which would require an encyclopedia not a chapter, I will endeavour to point out those salient features which are most characteristic, most distinctive or unusual. It might be helpful to keep one thumb in the 'grape variety' section of Chapter VI, and the right hand in the glossary (Appendix i).

The arrangement is by country, by district and by type. Good, bad and indifferent vintages are listed, and finally, in chart form, there is a breakdown of wines into dry, sweet, light and heavy.

If the structure is somewhat rigid and the generalisations too broad, I nevertheless feel that some guidance is better than no guidance at all. As tasting is so subjective, it is up to you, the reader, to develop your own pattern of knowledge and to clothe it with your own tasting experiences.

Red Bordeaux

Claret is thought of as a light table wine. It can however vary from deep coloured and heavy to 'clairet', palish and light, depending on district, vintage weather, vineyard site and vinification.

MEDOC

The classic claret area: firm dry wines, purple and tannic when young, elegant and harmonious when mature. Life-span depends on vintage, weight and class of wine. These are the main *communes:*

Pauillac

Depth and concentration of colour, opaque and purple when young; pronounced and concentrated *cabernet-sauvignon* aroma and flavour (see page 32), marked tannin and acidity when immature. The greatest wines for keeping and development. Home of three first growths.

St.-Estèphe

Deep colour; stark raw fruity nose, *cabernet* less marked; full, firm, tannic. Slow-developing, solid wines, from heavier clay soil.

St.-Julien

Copybook claret. Lighter; more cedary bouquet; balance, elegance, harmony. Not the longest-living but capable of great finesse.

Margaux

Quite variable in style but on the whole similar in colour and weight to St.-Julien; bouquet varietal, complex and fragrant. Develops well.

Moulis, Listrac, Soussans and St.-Laurent	These middle-Médoc and hinterland districts, noted mainly for good *bourgeois* growths, produce fruity and dry wines but without the strongly marked characteristics of greater districts and vineyards. Will keep, but not worth keeping too long.
Graves	Similar weight to Médoc but develops more quickly. Garnet coloured, showing earthy red-brown tinge sooner. Bouquet and flavour notably earthy, both being loose-knit, soft and rounded.
Pomerol	Two styles: one deep and firm but with full, silky *merlot* richness, slow developing; the other lighter in colour and weight; sweeter, more gentle and quick-maturing. Each style has a noticeably velvety texture in the mouth. Lighter vintages develop quickly.
St.-Emilion	Again has two styles: from the 'Côtes' around the town, deepish but quick-maturing wines, loose-knit, sweeter on bouquet and palate. Easy, flavoury. From the 'Graves' plateau next to Pomerol, firm fine fruity wines with depth of colour and flavour, with hint of iron/earth character detectable on nose and palate.
Fronsac	Good deep-coloured wines; hard, fruity bouquet and flavour, tannic and needing bottle-age though rarely capable of great development. Like a firm hard Pomerol. Austere but pure and characterful.
Bourg and Blaye	The poor man's Médoc – if I may so categorise without wishing to give offence. Dry, straightforward, rather coarse wines. Need a little bottle-age but not worth cellaring for ten years – all you will have is a still somewhat coarse minor wine, ten years older.
Claret vintages	*Great years:* 1928, 1929, 1945, 1947, 1949, 1953, 1959, 1961, 1966, 1970, 1975. *Good years:* 1933, 1934, 1943, 1948, 1950, 1952, 1955, 1962, 1964, 1971, 1976. *Indifferent or variable years:* 1937, 1954, 1957, 1958, 1960, some 1964, 1967, 1969, 1972, 1973, 1974. *Distinctly poor years:* 1951, 1956, 1963, 1965, 1968.
Maturity-span	*Great wines:* 12-30 years; *good wines:* 8-20; *lesser:* 5-10.

White Bordeaux

Ranges from very dry to medium-dry, from medium-sweet to very sweet; colour from very pale yellow-straw (more yellow in a hot vintage), golden-tinged with bottle-age, to the deep old-gold of venerable Sauternes. The common denominator on the nose is the soft 'lanolin' fragrance of the *sémillon* grape, fresh and mouth-watering when young, deep, rich, honeyed when fully mature.

Graves	Colour-range described above. Very dry to medium-dry, with more body and less of the mouth-puckering acidity of Loire whites, less fruity-fragrant than Hock. At best, refined; improves with five to ten years bottle-age. The less-than-best are often dull, stodgy uninspiring.
Sauternes	Deep, more golden in colour. Characteristic honeyed over-ripe grape smell from *pourriture noble*. Essentially sweet, luscious and full-bodied though varying in weight and richness, depending on year, and neatly

counter-balanced by acidity. Note particularly the concentration and aftertaste of the really great wines. Fine Sauternes not only keep well, they really need bottle-age (see below). An under-rated district.

Barsac Similar in style and purpose though sometimes paler, green-tinged when young; often more refreshingly forthcoming bouquet; slightly lighter in body and less rich, particularly in minor vintages.

White Bordeaux vintages *Great classic years:* 1921, 1928, 1937, 1945, 1947, 1949, 1955, 1959.
Good years: 1929, 1934, 1943, 1948, 1950, 1952, 1953, 1962, 1967, 1970, 1975.
Fairly good, slightly lighter years: 1957, 1961, 1966, 1969, 1971, 1973.
Variable or poor years: 1951, 1956, 1963, 1964, 1965, 1968, 1972, 1974.

Maturity-span *Great Sauternes:* 10 to 100 years; at peak 20 to 30. *Good Sauternes:* 8 to 40; at peak 10 to 20. *Lesser wines:* 3 to 10; peak 4 to 8. (The finest Graves of great vintages have a 10 to 30 year old span; even longer).

Burgundy, red

It is extremely difficult to generalise about burgundies. Often the dominant factor is a grower's or merchant's style. Nevertheless burgundy is essentially different in style, weight and development from claret, and subject to great variations of colour and body (and quality). At best, deep, rich colour, fine ripe *pinot* aroma and fragrance, fairly alcoholic yet velvety, and quicker-developing thanks to a lack of tannic astringency, the result of grape variety and vinification methods.

COTE DE NUITS The main classic red burgundy area producing at best full, firm long-lasting wines. By *commune*:

Gevrey-Chambertin At its best – good vintage, great vineyard, top grower – deep coloured, inimitable bouquet: rich, masculine, complex, with 'meaty' *pinot* aroma; full-bodied, firm yet velvety and long-lasting.

Chambolle-Musigny Almost the opposite: lighter, more gentle, feminine, elegant; noted for fragrance of bouquet. The 'Margaux' of the Côte de Nuits.

Morey-St.-Denis Two styles: one big and fruity, the other lighter and looser textured. At best firm and elegant. Sometimes 'fluffy' and short lived.

Vougeot The famous Clos is much sub-divided, and variable. Hope for a fairly full, firm, flavoury long-lasting wine.

Echézeaux Just above Vougeot, more close-knit and elegant; refined, some delicacy.

Vosne-Romanée The centre, the heart of the Côte de Nuits. Colour variable in depth; bouquet rich, fragrant and capable of extraordinary opulence, even spicy. On the palate, deep, rich, velvety but not heavy. At best the epitome of burgundian elegance and style.

Nuits-St.-Georges and Prémaux At best 'copybook', but without the majesty of Chambertin or regal opulence of Vosne-Romanée. Agreeable, fullish, firm, flavoury wines. Note the smoky-oak reminiscent *pinot* aroma and flavour of some of the finer *domaines*.

[45]

COTE DE BEAUNE	Generally more loose-grained, less concentrated and shorter life-span than Nuits. Easy and agreeable, but as with all burgundy, only the best *domaines* will give a true picture of the *pinot* grape and district styles. *Commune* names follow:
Aloxe-Corton	No more than pleasant, medium-weight wines except for Le Corton and the top vineyards which sometimes match Chambertin in weight with full, meaty, slightly roasted *pinot* aroma and flavour. Long-lasting.
Beaune	The centre, geographically and in style. At best, not too full, a certain elegance, good *pinot* flavour and balance.
Pommard	Not dissimilar, but in Epenots and Rugiens produces very distinguished, fruity wines which develop well.
Volnay	Lighter in colour and style; firm, elegant, a certain delicacy. The Chambolle-Musigny of the Côte de Nuits, but lower keyed.
Santenay	The most southerly of the Côtes, and relatively minor. True Santenay is light in colour and frankly no more than pleasant. Do not expect great depth or finesse.
Red Burgundy vintages	*Great years:* 1911, 1915, 1919, 1923, 1928, 1945, 1947, 1949, 1959, 1969, 1971. *Good years:* 1924, 1926, 1929, 1933, 1934, 1937, 1948, 1952, 1953, 1955, 1961, 1962, 1964, 1966, 1967, 1970, 1976. *Fairly good years:* 1954, 1957, 1972, 1973, 1974. *Poor years:* 1951, 1956, 1958, 1960, 1963, 1965, 1968, 1975.
Maturity-span	*Great wines:* 8-30 years. *Good wines:* 6-15. *Lesser wines:* 3-8. (Some top-class wines of the 1920's are still most attractive. It is hard to generalise.)

White Burgundy

	Virtually all white burgundy is pale in colour, and dry. Exceptionally hot vintage years, like 1959 and 1964, will produce a deeper colour, more body and very slight sweetness. But wine from top-class vineyards in other fine ripe vintages may also have more colour and richness.
Chablis	Noted for its appealing pale straw-yellow colour with greenish tinge; firm, steely bouquet; and in particular, for its dryness and crisp, rapier-like, quality: austere yet subtle and long-flavoured.
Puligny-Montrachet	In weight and style not unlike Chablis but the best have a noticeable and very fragrant smoky *chardonnay* aroma. Firm, crisp, refreshing on the palate. 'Copybook' white burgundy.
Le Montrachet	Rich yellow colour, shot with gold as it matures; deep, complex, rich 'smoky' bouquet. Dry, rich, complex, long flavour, fragrant after-taste.
Bâtard-	Fine full dry, oaky. Substantial and of high quality.
Chevalier-	More refined, lighter, elegant. Fine quality.
Chassagne-Montrachet	Not unlike its neighbouring *commune*, Puligny, but perhaps slightly less elegant, less austere. (Also produces excellent red wine.)

Meursault	Often yellower in colour; fine bouquet; broader texture and character.
Corton-Charlemagne	Noted for its full, nutty, vanilla-oak aroma and flavour. Full-bodied, long-lasting.
White Burgundy vintages	*Great years:* 1952, 1967, 1969, 1971. *Good years:* 1953, 1955, 1959, 1961, 1962, 1964, 1966, 1970, 1974. *Moderate years:* 1957, 1972, 1973, 1975. *Poor years:* 1956, 1958, 1960, 1963, 1965, 1968.

South Burgundy

South of the Côte d'Or, between Chagny and the outskirts of Lyon, are a string of relatively minor districts producing pleasing, fairly distinctive but not particularly distinguished wines.

Chalonnais	Rully and Mercurey make stylish medium-light red wines of a generally burgundian character; fruity, and best drunk fairly young. Montagny makes good, well-balanced dry white wine, pleasing but not great.
Mâconnais	Mâcon rouge and Mâcon blanc are at best agreeable clean, wholesome, lightish red and dry white. Do not expect more. Pouilly-Fuissé, though a cut above, has been much over-regarded and over-priced. At best it is pale, dry, clean and crisp. No great subtleties or memorable distinctions.
Beaujolais	There are two sorts of genuine Beaujolais: the currently fashionable, modern-vinified wines which take a lead from *beaujolais nouveau*. Their characteristics are a palish, pink-red colour; very pronounced, almost scented *gamay* aroma; dry, very light (thin in poorer years), flavoury and with marked, refreshing acidity. To be drunk young. However, the finest, worth seeking out, are still the unblended single-vineyard wines made by older methods: deeper and more substantial in colour and body, with a deep elegant vinous *gamay* bouquet and flavour, better with some bottle-age. (Not to be confused with the plummy, stewed, characterless commercial 'grocer's' beaujolais.) Beaujolais blanc is usually pale and dry, often with slightly more body than Mâcon blanc or even Pouilly-Fuissé.
Beaujolais vintages	*The rare recent classic years:* 1967, 1969, 1970, 1971, 1973, 1976. Avoid poor years. Though made every year it is not good every year. Beaujolais *can* be thin, feeble and bitter. Much has been, of late, undistinguished and over-priced.

Rhône Red

The main characteristics of the Rhône reflect the nature of the terrain, and sun. Full-coloured, deep and very purple when young; full, heavy, alcoholic, less elegant, less acidity than burgundy. Bouquet the least interesting feature.

Châteauneuf-du-Pape	Most people's idea of a Rhône wine: deep coloured (unless poor year or speedy vinification), four-square, hefty, fruity, soft yet good balance. Bouquet vinous, but no strong varietal aroma owing to the *mélange* of grapes. Tannin and acidity less marked than in claret.

Hermitage	Although deep and purple when young, a contrast to Châteauneuf in style: less heavy, with finer bouquet, considerable fruit, more refinement, and balance. Sometimes claret-like. Improves with maturity.
Côte Rôtie	Some of the weight and 'heat' of Châteauneuf, with the style and elegance of Hermitage. Fine long-lasting wines.
Lirac, Ventoux Gigondas	Although from the hot southern Rhône, making lighter, almost beaujolais-like wines, at best delightful, fruity and not too serious; often lacking depth and finesse.
Tavel Rosé	The nearest rosé to a red wine. Tavel's most notable feature is its dryness, body and certain austerity. Less frivolous than most rosés.

Rhône White

Geographical position gives clue to weight and character. Palish in colour, more body than white burgundies, and less acidity. Bouquet not very marked save for really good Hermitage blanc and Château Grillet.

Châteauneuf-du-Pape blanc	Not often seen, but in a good year slightly sweet and with unusual character. Fullish in colour and body; deep and rich.
Hermitage blanc	A lemon-tinged straw colour; a squeeze of lemon peel in the often stylish bouquet and flavour. Dry, often refined.
Château Grillet	Unusual, and deserving its unique appellation. In a good year (1969 for example) deep yellow in colour; vinous, rich slightly smoky bouquet; dryish, fairly full, rich, stylish, original, slightly caramel-tinged flavour.
Rhône vintages	*Very good years:* 1929, 1949, 1952, 1953, 1955, 1957, 1959, 1960, 1961, 1962, 1964, 1966, 1967, 1969, 1970. *Moderate years:* 1971, 1972, 1974. *Poor years:* 1956, 1963, 1965, 1968, 1975.

Loire

Total contrast to Rhône. Mainly white, very dry to medium-dry; much lighter in body, with pronounced refreshing acidity.

Sancerre and Pouilly-Fumé	Both pale, slightly green-tinged; marked, piquant, raw blackcurrant *sauvignon blanc* aroma; very dry, light (thin in poor years), a piquant fruitiness and high acidity. Somewhat over-fashionable.
Vouvray	Although with high acidity, much broader in style than Sancerre, with pleasant, not very pronounced, waxy-vanilla aroma. Both dry and medium-sweet (*demi-sec*). The latter can be long-lasting, developing honeyed richness. Also pleasing *pétillant* and fully sparkling wines.
Saumur	Thin but flavoury whites and red (Champigny). Excellent sparkling wines, lively with attractive grapey aroma, medium-dry, light and clean.
Chinon and Bourgeuil	The two main red wine districts. Medium, beaujolais-like colour: violet when young. Marked piquant raspberry-like aroma. Dry, light, very flavoury, piquant and fruity, but tart and thin in lesser years.

[48]

Savennières	Yellow; elegant waxy bouquet; dry, firm, elegant and finely balanced.
Coteaux du Layon	Yellow; rather underplayed 'lanolin' aroma that deepens and improves with age. Main features: semi-sweetness, rich ripe attractive fruitiness, and marked acidity. Bonnézeaux and Quarts-de-Chaume keep magnificently, indeed need bottle-age. Good summer dessert wines.
Muscadet	Near to nondescript in colour and bouquet; pretty low-keyed in flavour too. Main feature bone dryness, but clean, zestful, the best refined.
Loire vintages	*Great classic years:* 1921, 1937, 1947, 1953, 1964. *Good years:* 1969, 1970, 1971, 1973, 1974. (Only the finest Vouvrays and Coteaux du Layon will last 15 years or more. The very dry whites are thin and over-acid in the poorer vintages and do not keep well).

Alsace

In Alsace, the wines are named after grape variety and not district. Virtually all are white, most are dry; overall honest and reliable.

Riesling	Main feature: firm fruit, and steeliness of flavour; dry, crisp acidity.
Gewürztraminer	Main feature: spicy-grapey bouquet and flavour. Soft, fatter, less acid.
Muscat	Assertive grapey bouquet, but surprisingly dry, light, sometimes austere.
Tokay, Pinot	Distinctive dry wines but overshadowed by the first two classic grapes.
Sylvaner	Lower-keyed, less pronounced characteristics. Dry, mild.
Alsace vintages	*Good years:* 1966, 1967, 1969, 1970, 1971, 1973. *Thin years:* 1963, 1965, 1968, 1972 1976.

Champagne

All-important is the name of the *marque*, though most major champagne houses produce a *de-luxe* blend of some refinement and distinction. Whether the full, 'meaty' classics (like Krug and Bollinger) or pale, light *blanc de blancs* (Taittinger for example) the essential characteristics of a fine champagne are:

Appearance: appealing palish colour with a steady, continuous flow of small, evenly-spaced bubbles. With age the colour deepens to gold, sparkle less lively.

Bouquet: the next major feature is a firm vinous bouquet, with either a rich meaty style or a nutty, smoky-charred *pinot chardonnay* aroma.

Palate: bone dry to dryish; light and firm to full, depending on the house style. What distinguishes fine champagne from other sparkling wines is finesse, elegance, length of flavour and crisp, positive finish.

Champagne vintages	*Old classic years:* 1923, 1928, 1937, 1943, 1945, 1947, 1949, 1952, 1953. *More recent years:* 1955, 1959, 1961, 1962, 1964, 1966, 1969, 1970, 1971.

Cahors

Although recently up-graded, the wines from this famous old area are rarely seen outside France, and the 'black' Cahors almost never. At best deep characterful substantial reds, soft, fullish, long-lasting.

Midi

The Gard, Hérault, and Aude areas produce a vast amount of white and red – but not for the connoisseur to linger over. At best they make agreeable table wines. Some, like Fitou, have character and flavour.

Vins-doux-naturels However, perhaps the most interesting, but little seen outside France, are the classic *vins doux:* 'muted' sweet dessert wines such as Lunel, Muscat de Frontignan, and (in the Rhône) Beaumes de Venise. All have a palish tawny-brown colour; attractive, muscatelle-grapey aroma; sweet, fullish but not heavy like port: easy, raisiny-flavoured wines with refreshing end acidity.

Provence

Solid, respectable but stodgy reds; dry rather unexciting whites; and dry rather zestless rosés, the main attraction being a fancy bottle. Fine for drinking on the spot. Affords the peripatetic wine lover happy explorations to discover the occasional outstanding *domaine*, such as Ott and Vignelaure. Bandol reds can be good.

Jura

Frankly, the red, white, rosé and sparkling wines from this area, with a few exceptions, are sound, quite appealing but commercial and fairly undistinguished. The Jura is, however, the cradle of one of the most original wines in the world: the *vin jaune* of Château-Chalon. Yellow in colour, with strange nutty bouquet; dry, austere, fairly full-bodied: a cross between an old fino sherry and tokay szamorodni.

The white wine of Étoile is very dry, straw-flavoured and of good quality. Nearby, Château d'Arlay makes dry white wine of rare distinction.

Germany

From the point of view of the connoisseur, German wines are white, ranging from dry and light to exceptionally sweet and rich; in quality and style between insubstantial and short, to deep, rich, refined, and long-flavoured. There is much pleasant commercial wine.

The range, thanks to oenology and the new German wine laws, is infinitely less varied than before. Real character and real quality depend on dedicated growers and estates. Happily, there are still quite a few left.

Fruity-acidity The essential thing to bear in mind is that the German wine-makers' ideal is 'fruity-acidity': a combination of delicacy, ripe-grapey quality, fragrance and refreshing acidity. However, thanks to advanced wine-making techniques and a rather contrived efficiency, quality standards are evening out and the grape style, sweetness and consistency seem to mask district, soil, micro-climate and other local variations. Perhaps the 'ideal' is now too easily reached at the expense of character and individuality. Nevertheless, the great estates in the classic areas continue to produce fine wines. Quality and vintage variations are still very important.

Qualities	The connoisseur will concern himself with the clearly defined fine wines (*Qualitätswein-mit-Prädikat*): *Kabinett:* natural, unsugared wines of a recognised quality. *Spätlese:* late-picked, i.e. ripe grapes. Intensity, weight, character and sweetness vary from district to district, grower to grower, year to year, but very generally speaking, palish in colour, dry to medium-dry. *Auslese:* from selected riper bunches. As with *spätlesen*, variations of sweetness and body depend on place and vintage. *Auslese* wine is richer, riper, usually, but not necessarily, sweeter, and of fine quality. *Beerenauslese:* from singly-selected very ripe grapes. Usually a fuller yellow-gold in colour; most characteristic bouquet: rich, ripe, honeyed scent of *edelfäule*. On the palate: sweet, fullish, rich, ripe, often grapey, with fine balancing acidity. Becomes softer and more complex with age. Long-lasting. *Trockenbeerenauslese:* from select, over-ripe, shrivelled grapes. Yellow-gold, deepening to fine old gold with age; concentrated essence-of-grapes aroma, often raisiny but when immature less assertive than the smell of *beerenauslesen*. Very sweet, very rich, highly concentrated; very often with low alcoholic content but high degrees of sugar and acidity. The world's rarest and richest dessert wines. Very long-lasting.
Rheingau	*Riesling* reigns supreme in this district and produces fine, firm, steely wines with intense bouquet and fragrance; dry to medium-dry, long finish. Also, in suitably fine years, outstanding dessert wines with incredible concentration, richness and refinement. Long-lasting. Districts provide thematic variations, for example Eltville wines are light but firm and elegant, Rauenthal rich almost spicy, Hochheim masculine, four-square, perhaps more earthy.
Rheinhesse	Generally softer, more 'open', less condensed, attractive ripe fruity wines.
Pfalz (Palatinate)	Germany's most southerly great wine district, just north of Alsace. Essentially more substantial, deep grapey wines. Even the dry *rieslings* have a touch more body and richness; the more old-fashioned Pfalz wines have a weight and earthiness of their own.
Nahe	Most noticeable characteristics of the finer qualities: fruit-salad bouquet; firm, medium-light, crisp-bodied. Can be quite dry. Half-way, geographically and in style, between the Rheingau and Moselle.
Moselle	Usually pale, green-tinged and often *spritzig* (very slight effervescence); fruity, light, 'high-toned' *riesling* aroma; dry to medium-dry, usually light, low in alcohol, but enormously appealing with its characteristic refreshing acidity. In exceptional years, *beerenauslese* and *trockenbeeren-auslese* quality wines made.

Saar/Ruwer	In essence, Moselle in style. Special characteristics: peach-like bouquet; often very dry and with fine, steely acidity, delicacy and subtlety. Thin, verging on tartness in lesser years.
Baden	To the east of Alsace, Baden produces a large quantity of wine, both commercial and good, though rarely of fine, quality. Rather four-square in style; agreeable bouquet and flavour but relatively undistinguished, unsubtle and lacking zest. The reds are not very full in colour, lacking the character and firmness of their French counterparts.
Franconia (Würzburg)	Known generally as Steinwein: fine dry steely wines from Würzburg, like *grand cru* Chablis, yet with germanic fruit and acidity. Sylvaner also thrives here producing wines of unusual firmness and quality.
German vintages	*Great years:* 1949, 1953, 1959, 1964, 1969, 1971, 1975. *Good years:* 1955, 1961, 1966, 1967, 1976. *Light years:* 1962, 1970, 1973. *Poor, thin years:* 1956, 1960, 1963, 1965, 1968, 1972.

Austria

Although there is a family resemblance, it is a mistake to compare Austrian whites with German Rhine wines. They look similar, have variations of a delicate grapey bouquet and are lightish in style but soft edged, the fine wines lacking that distinguishing fruity-acidity and length. The *grüner-veltliner* grape grown in the Wachau district typifies the soft, easy Austrian style. High quality dessert wines, *beeren* and *trockenbeeren-auslesen* are made, but again, though good, often lack the length and breed of the German equivalent.

Some top-class individual growers and commercial firms. Worthy of greater attention, and good value.

Hungary

This once most characterful and varied wine country is now dominated by co-operatives and State marketing. Doubtless overall quality has improved; certainly the wines are good value. But how can anything great be produced if the pursuit of excellence is not encouraged and individual effort goes unrewarded?

Table wines	A far wider range than Austria, but amongst the table wines the whites are best though the highest quality they are allowed to aspire to is the equivalent of *spät-auslese*. Look out for softness, almost milkiness of bouquet and flavour. The famous reds from Eger are robust and assertive but lack finesse – ideal for paprika dishes.
Tokay	One area stands out; it is one of the unique classic wine areas of the world. Tokay: *Szamorodni:* the natural white wine of the region. Pale yellow in colour, characteristic appley nose of the *furmint* grape, either quite dry or slightly sweet. Unusual flavour, fullish, quite good length.

Aszu: ranges in colour from straw to deep yellow, golden-tinged with age. Pronounced appley nose, unlike any other wine aroma. Graduations of sweetness up from two *puttonyos* slightly sweet, three '*putts*' roughly medium-sweet, four and five '*putts*' rich dessert wines. Fairly full-bodied but not heavy; rich, curiously attractive appley flavour, good acidity and finish.

Essence: no longer made for sale though an *aszu-essencia*, somewhat on a par with the former six *puttonyos*, is now marketed. Like a rich *aszu* but more luscious and concentrated.

Tokay essence of old vintages varies from deep amber to deep tawny and has a very heavy sediment; a magnificent concentrated, raisiny almost pungent nose (a cross between old Malmsey and a *trockenbeerenauslese*); very sweet on the palate, rich, concentrated, with high acidity and penetrating, lingering flavour and aromatic aftertaste. They appear to have unlimited life.

Italy

An immense range of wines: all shades of colour, type and strength. Although quality can be high, connoisseurs' interest, as in California, tends to be local except for the universally acknowledged classics.

Chianti

Made from four grapes, the balance, as in Bordeaux, can vary from district to district and year to year. What are the distinguishing features? Firstly, a rich garnet hue, deep when young, warm brick-red when mature; secondly, a deep, slightly earthy, and complex flavour with a characteristic 'upturned' finish: tannic and slightly bitter.

Brunello

Brunello di Montalcino is widely regarded as one of, if not the greatest of, Italian reds. Of the chianti family, but very deep brown-purple in colour, a 'hot' concentrated aroma and flavour and swingeing finish. Immense keeping power and longevity. The Mouton/Latour of the Florence-Siena region, with price to match.

Barolo

The favourite amongst English connoisseurs, possibly because it is nearest to their idea of a classic red. Characteristics: fine deep colour, fruit and finesse on nose and palate; full-bodied, yet finely balanced. Tannic when young, needs ageing, keeps well.

Valpolicella

A lighter, elegant red from near Verona.

Soave

One of the best-known dry whites. They used to be yellow and flat owing to over-maturing in cask. Now they are fresher and altogether more pleasant and reliable.

Marsala

One of the classic fortified wines of the world; deep, plummy-purple when young; sweet, meaty – almost malty – nose; very sweet, full, rich, earthy/volcanic burnt flavour, with a tangy-acid, sometimes slightly bitter, finish.

Portugal

A wide range of table wines, many with character and above-ordinary quality. The following are the main districts and styles:

Minho
Vinho verde can be white or red. Both are light, with slight to marked effervescent prickle and very high acidity that can be raw, thin, even tart in the wrong context. Commercial wines are slightly sweeter, acidity toned down.

Madura
Not a district: 'mature' white wine, heavy and flat-tasting – strange to modern taste buds.

Dão
Reliable reds and whites, the latter sound but rather dull and lacking character. The best red Dão is full in colour and body, with positive bouquet – classic, but a little earthy – and fine flavour and finish.

Colares
Red, rare, and worth seeking out. They hold colour and age well; deep meaty nose; rich but not heavy in style.

Setúbal
The Moscatel de Setúbal is an old classic grapey dessert wine. Pale tawny-brown in colour; light, clear muscatel-grape aroma and flavour; sweet of course, but not heavy.

PORT
All port is fortified with brandy, full-bodied and with a high alcoholic content. Most port is sweet. These are the main styles:

Ruby
Should be full and true ruby in colour; fruity 'peppery' nose, not unlike young vintage port; invariably sweet, full and fruity. Tends to be strapping and hefty.

Tawny
A true tawny, aged in the wood, is surprisingly pale in colour, an attractive amber-tawny hue, with positive, sometimes lemon-yellow, rim; its next most noticeable feature is the soft nutty (cobnuts, brazils) bouquet – sweet and harmonious. Invariably sweet on the palate but not heavy, indeed usually lightish, with gently rich, soft but nutty, extended flavour, and fine aftertaste. Lesser tawnies lack these characteristics.

White
Palish, yellow-tinged; nose somewhat characterless; rarely truly dry, usually medium-dry and a trifle heavy and dull. Pleasant though lacking the freshness of sherry and the rich tang of a dry madeira. Serve cold.

Vintage port
Style depends on the vintage, age, and on the shipper's house-style. Quality is reliably high amongst the major shippers.

Young vintage port is deep, very purple, often opaque; rather peppery, alcoholic and unyielding on the nose; very sweet, very full-bodied, fruity but slightly rasping.

Mature vintage port will have shed its colour and become medium-deep, much more tawny-hued; the bouquet will have ripened and developed overtones, sometimes liquorice-like. When very old the fruit fades leaving the brandy exposed. The maturing wine dries out, becoming lighter in body, softer and more harmonious. Styles range from Noval—generally soft, light, feminine and forward—to Taylor—full, with firm 'backbone', great power, depth and longevity.

Port vintages	*Generally 'declared' vintages:* 1896, 1900, 1904, 1908, 1912, 1920, 1924, 1927, 1934, 1935, 1945, 1947, 1948, 1955, 1960, 1963, 1966, 1970, 1975. *Lighter or limited declaration vintages:* 1911, 1917, 1922, 1931, 1942, 1950, 1954, 1958, 1962, 1967.
Maturity-span	*Great classics:* 12 to 120 years, at peak 15-40. *Good vintages:* 12-30 years.

Madeira

	One of the three really great and traditional fortified wines of the world. Range: fairly dry to very sweet. Essential characteristics, rich burnt tangy bouquet and flavour, and fairly high acidity. The rare top-quality wines have remarkable longevity. Basic styles named after grapes:
Sercial	The palest, deep 'fino' yellow, sometimes amber; the freshest, most mouth-watering, aroma, but still with burnt-tangy character; dry to medium-dry, the lightest, but still with a fair amount of body.
Verdelho	Varying amber-brown shades; nose deeper, richer, more tangy; medium-dry to medium-sweet, medium-full bodied, fairly rich attractive tangy wine with good acidity.
Bual	Deeper, warm oloroso-type amber-brown; rich, more 'volcanic', 'meaty' and assertive madeira tang; sweet, rich, fine-flavoured.
Malmsey	Like Bual but sweeter and softer, with a rather more grapey-rich flavour added to the burnt volcanic character. Intensely rich and attractive.
Old vintage and old solera	The many authentic old solera and vintage madeiras have a common denominator: great richness of colour, powerful bouquet and length of flavour. A true old madeira has a positive tawny-brown colour, with ruddy hue in the middle and pronounced greeny-amber rim; strong burnt aroma, high acidity; sometimes sweetness fades, but maintains rich, complex flavour, with extraordinarily powerful tang and extended finish.
Life-span	Longest-living after Tokay essence: 100 years or more.

Spain

	The mass of Spanish table wine, red and white, is of ordinary to good commercial quality. Reds range from light to fairly full; whites are less appealing, the aroma of some being positively unattractive. Few will engage the attention of the connoisseur, though some do deserve it.
Rioja	The major region producing wines of quality and style, particularly the reds which are of Bordeaux type but often more supple and attractive than all but the best young claret. Fairly deep in colour; agreeable, fruity, sometimes classic, almost cedary, aroma; dry but not over-tannic, pleasant medium-weight, soft through cask-age; fine balance and flavour.
SHERRY	Basically dry white wine, but with a wide range of styles within the two basic 'families': fino and oloroso. The former are usually dry and the latter, though starting dry, generally have sweetening wine blended in.

Fino	Characteristics: paleness of colour, fine lemon-straw-yellow; refined, positive fresh *flor* aroma (less marked on lower quality wines); dry, light, fresh, with long crisp finish. Not very alcoholic.
Manzanilla	A fino from Sanlucar, usually very dry and with a fine tangy flavour.
Amontillado	Deeper in colour; light amber-brown. Fine quality amontillados have a very slight fino-reminiscent smell but are richer and distinctly nutty. Dry to medium-dry, slightly fuller in body and nutty flavoured.
Palo cortado	A rarer and refined version of amontillado, similar colour and weight; dryish but a certain richness, nuttiness, vinosity and length of flavour.
Oloroso	Total contrast to fino: deeper in colour, ranging from deep amber to warm amber-brown; complete absence of *flor* tang; softer, sweeter on nose and palate. Medium to full-bodied. A mid-morning or after-dinner dessert wine.
Cream	An extension of oloroso, sometimes paler; certainly very sweet and soft.
Brown	Now almost totally out of fashion. Deep and brown in colour, with a burnt oloroso aroma; very sweet, heavy.
Pedro Ximenez	The ultimate brown sherry: opaque colour; powerful tangy, burnt-grapes aroma; very sweet, heavy, highly concentrated but fine acidity. Magnificent in its way but rarely offered commercially now.

United States

CALIFORNIA	The scale, variety and quality of Californian wines are not to be underestimated: red, white, rosé, sparkling, fortified and 'flavoured'; mass-produced, sound, commercial, refined, even rarefied. Amongst the fine wines, grape variety takes precedence over area, though the Napa Valley is undoubtedly the 'Mecca'. Other districts are also known to possess actual or potential 'classic' vineyards. The wine maker is all-important.
Cabernet-sauvignon	The finest red, widely planted. Tends to be used alone, unblended. Characteristics more consistently deep coloured than in Bordeaux, often opaque and very purple when young, maintains its depth of colour better than claret with age; often a pronounced blackcurrant, recognisably *cabernet*, aroma but usually with earthy/volcanic overtones; slightly less dry in character than claret, often very full-bodied, hefty wines full of fruit and quite tannic. Can be magnificent; very long-lasting.
Zinfandel	Unique to California: variable, but mainly satisfactory red, not unlike *cabernet* in weight, style, character and longevity. Possibly nearest to a Barolo in style.
Pinot	Not to be compared with burgundy. *Pinot* in California produces a fullish coloured, full-bodied rich rounded wine but with a 'stewed' and earthy quality, almost totally devoid of the classic *pinot* aroma and flavour. Nevertheless it can be rich and fine and long-lasting.
Chardonnay	Outstandingly the most successful varietal in terms of true classic style. Colour usually palish to pronounced yellow; remarkable *chardonnay*

aroma: oak vanilla tang, richness and freshness; dry, never very light –
more like a Corton-Charlemagne or Bâtard-Montrachet in weight and
style. The best have a remarkably clean true flavour and quality, length
and aftertaste.

**Johannisberg
riesling**

Palish, fairly fruity, medium-dry and of general Germanic character but
of course lacking the inimitable freshness and fruity-acidity of a Rheingau.
However, some fine wines being made in Napa and Livermore,
occasionally of spätlese quality.

**Emerald
riesling**

Pale, clean attractive grapey aroma; medium-dry, fairly light, clean and
fruity. Not a refined wine but consistently attractive.

Fumé-blanc

Although not absolutely comparable with the light acidic Blanc Fumé of
the Loire, nevertheless a successful version: pale; refreshing, fruity
aroma; dry, appetizing and with crisp finish.

Gewurztraminer

Some of the spicyness and softness of the Alsace prototype but lacking
complexity and delicacy. Plenty of flavour.

Napa vintages

Exceptional years: 1941, 1951, 1958, 1959, 1964, 1966, 1968, 1970, 1973,
1974. *Good years:* 1955, 1960, 1961, 1965, 1975. *Moderate years:* 1962,
1963, 1967, 1969, 1971, 1972, 1976.

NEW YORK

One vineyard stands out, making the best hock-style wines in
North America: Dr. Frank's *Johannisberg riesling* being outstanding,
and true in character and quality.

Australia

To the older generation of Englishmen, Australian wine conjures up an
iron-tonic 'Burgundy'-type wine sold in flagons. The scene in Australia is
totally different, the technology and enthusiasm resembling those of
California but with far older traditions.

The range of styles and qualities is enormous. The practice of many
big commercial producers, as well as small wineries, to produce a wide
range, blending from different grapes and different regions, adds to the
profusion – and confusion.

Hunter Valley

Perhaps the oldest classic district, in New South Wales, north of Sydney.
The home of the *shiraz*, producing a rich, earthy Burgundy/Rhône-style
wine with the most evocative of all aromas: 'sweaty saddle'; also of the
semillon, less interesting dry whites, and, a recent development, of the rare
chardonnay (Tyrrell and Max Lake producing two outstanding examples).
Other great producers include McWilliams and the ubiquitous
Lindeman's; and smart new wineries like Rothbury.

Barossa

A vast and hugely successful wine valley in South Australia, north of
Adelaide, with long-established family businesses like Yalumba and
precocious newcomers like Wolf Blass; the enormous Kaiserstuhl co-
operative (excellent *rieslings*), Seppeltsfield (fortified wines); Saltrams
and Orlando (producing *rieslings* of outstanding quality).

Clare/Watervale	Also north of Adelaide, growing *cabernet*, *shiraz*, *rieslings* and making good *flor* sherries. Wineries: Quelltaler, Chateau Clare (new), Stanley Leasingham, Sevenhills.
Southern Vales	To the south of Adelaide, small family wineries like D'aremberg Osborne, Kay's Amery; large wineries like Seaview, Hardy's (making magnificent ports) and the old Chateau Reynella, all growing and making a wide range of wines.
Coonawarra	An astonishing strip of red earth in the middle of nowhere, first planted early this century, only lately recognised as the *Médoc* of Australia; magnificent *cabernets* and *shiraz* reds, some good *rieslings* produced by Wynn's, Brand's Laira winery, Redman's.
Rutherglen and N. E. Victoria	An old classic area making a variety of wines, but famed for its magnificent rich tangy *muscats*, the great classic dessert wines of Australia. Best producers: Morris's, Chambers' Rosewood, All Saints and Bailey's Bundarra. Browns at Milawa produce a fine range including excellent *rhine-rieslings* and *shiraz*.
Chateau Tahbilk	Nearer to Melbourne and worthy of special mention. Very old winery producing *marsanne*, *semillon*, *shiraz* and top quality (when mature) *cabernet-sauvignon*.

South Africa

Perhaps the most beautiful of all winelands, the Cape, once the home of the most famous dessert wines, went into a long decline and has only relatively recently pulled out. Now famed mainly for its excellent sherries (thanks to the outstanding technology of the omni-present co-operative, the KWV) some fine wines are now being made – magnificent *rieslings* at Nederberg and interesting reds at individual estates. The most at-home white is the *steen*, steely, fine; and, of the reds, the *shiraz*, an unusual style for the English palate, not unlike its Australian counterpart. *Cabernet* has not yet achieved real distinction, but there are interesting developments.

England

The resurgence of English vineyards has been remarkable. Pioneered by Sir Guy Salisbury-Jones and the late Colonel and Mrs. Gore-Browne in the 1950s, small vineyards now abound in Southern England, the best sweeping from Norfolk in the east to Wiltshire in the west.

Müller-Thurgau	Several early-ripening white grapes are grown amongst which *müller-thurgau* consistently makes the most attractive wines, *seyval* or *seyve-villard* also being popular. District styles have not yet clearly emerged, but top vineyards – making better and more interesting wines than many competitors in the Loire and other northerly European districts – include Pilton Manor, Magdalen Rivaner, Lamberhurst Priory, Adgestone and Felstar.

	very light	light	medium-light
very dry		Muscadet, Sancerre, Pouilly-Blanc Fumé, Bourgeuil	Chablis, MANZANILLA, ← Champagne ↕ →, Chinon, Savennières
dry	Saar-Ruwer, ←Beaujolais→, Vinho Verde ↕	Saumur-Champigny, Saumur, Nahe, Nahe Spätlesen, Mâcon blanc, Rully, Santenay, Gigondas, ←Pomerol→, Vouvray, Lirac, Côtes de Ventoux	FINO ↕, Steinwein (Würzburg) ↕, Puligny-Montrachet, Chevalier-Montrachet, Chassagne-Montrachet, Montagny, Listrac, Moulis, Mâcon rouge, Provence rosé, Riesling (Alsace), Mercurey, Steen (S. Africa), Fumé-blanc (U.S.A.), Tokay d'Alsace, Beaujolais blanc, Pinot d'Alsace, Tavel rosé, Muscat d'Alsace, Meursault, Rheingau Kabinett, and Spätlesen ↕ →
medium-dry	←	mid-Moselle →, Moselle Spätlesen, Anjou rosé ↕	Rheinhessen Spätlesen, Emerald riesling (U.S.A.), ← Austrian whites ↕ →, Rheingau Auslesen
medium-sweet		Moselle Auslesen, Moscato d'Asti, Bonnézeaux	Rheinhessen Auslesen, Champagne demi-sec, Vouvray demi-sec
sweet			Coteaux du Layon, Moselle Beerenauslesen, Rheinhessen, Moselle Trockenbeerenauslesen
very sweet			

Key to type-faces: Red wine, *White wine*, RED FORTIFIED WINE, *WHITE FORTIFIED A*

Summary   I should like to end by making four points: first, that the wine lover should deliberately broaden his sights; secondly, in doing so, that he should make allowances for strange styles and flavours, and appreciate the context – for example rich food, hot climate – that certain wines were made for and taste best in; thirdly, as witnessed positively by Australia and California, and slightly negatively by South Africa and Hungary, wine is as good, as fine, as the wine drinker requires it to be, will pay for (or the State will allow). Positive, active, articulate connoisseurship *and* enthusiasm, allied to thriving economies (which allow healthy discretionary incomes) encourage the wine maker to excel up to a point. For, and this is the fourth point, with all the will in the world, *great* wines cannot be made in unsuitable areas, which is why the connoisseur always returns, in hope and with added appreciation, to the well-tried and long-established classics.

VIII: On tasting expertise

Although there is a marked difference between what is insipid and what pleases our taste, the interval is certainly not wide between what is acknowledged to be good and what is excellent. BRILLAT-SAVARIN The Physiology of Taste, 1825

Experience – and the novice

There are, I believe, two general but little-understood points concerning tasting ability, and they are related. First, the more one has tasted, the less clear-cut may be one's reactions and the less dogmatic one's pronouncements. This is because the experienced taster (almost always a professional) has been exposed to such a wide range of closely-related smells and tastes, and has met with so many exceptions to the rules. The corollary is an easily noted one: that the beginner and amateur having fresh perception and an uncluttered vinous memory, is frequently more certain of himself and sometimes more accurate in identification.

Guessing games

Second, a point which may probably be widely accepted but that is rarely admitted: the great 'guessing-game' experts almost always perform in the comparatively limited field of very fine wines and great vintages, the characteristics of which stand out in sharp black and white, compared with the half-tones of middle-quality wines or the bleak wash of the *ordinaires*. It is not uncommon for the highest scorers to be amateurs, for their greatest performances arc usually set in an even more limited (however excellent) context, that of their own and their friends' cellars.

I do not wish to decry the seasoned and discerning amateur palates, or spoil their fun. On the contrary, without such enthusiastic and enquiring interest, without lay scholarship, the precarious incentive to *produce* such wines would waver, to everyone's loss. I merely make these points to keep things in perspective.

Having cleared the ground, I would like to pursue the subject of tasting 'blind'.

Tasting blind

It is my firm opinion (one of the few these days unwhittled by doubts!) that to assess the qualities of a wine by tasting it completely blind, without any hint of what it might be, is the most useful and salutary discipline that any self-respecting taster can be given. It is not infrequently the most humiliating. The first thing it does is to concentrate the thoughts, and expose fresh and unprejudiced senses to the problem of analysing the colour, bouquet and flavour. To know what the wine is before one starts to taste is like reading the end of a detective novel first; it satisfies the curiosity but dampens the interest.

The occasion -

Should blind tastings and guessing games be conducted at the dinner table? This is perhaps the most vexed question of all. I am sure that my colleagues in the British wine trade, particularly fellow Masters of Wine, will be the first to agree that it is one of the hazards of their occupation to be expected to 'perform' before an anonymous-looking glass of wine, and before only too un-anonymous and hideously expectant hosts and fellow guests: to pronounce vineyard, vintage and the name of the cellar-master in ten seconds flat. It is not that it *cannot* be done, even in this time. It can, but only in rare and exceptional circumstances, and I exclude all known methods of cheating, like bribing the butler. The point is that unless there is an immediate and quite positive 'click' of recognition, the only alternative is an extremely elaborate round-the-houses process of elimination, an intellectual exercise that takes time and may well be acutely boring for those waiting and watching. At a dinner party, particularly, the surest way of offending one's hostess is to undergo these mental contortions, letting one's meal go cold, and possibly even delaying subsequent courses.

- and the company

Broad-minded professionals don't mind making fools of themselves in the company of others in the business. At least, they re-assure themselves, their friends in the trade *know* how really difficult it is to identify wines, and they all have comforting knowledge of their common manifold blunders. It is another thing to be exposed before, and caught out by, amateurs – perhaps their own customers – who simply don't understand the complexity and problems involved.

Dinner party tastings

I personally subscribe to 'blind' tasting, at least of the principal wines, at a dinner party, but only on the following conditions:

☐ that the occasion is an appropriate one – good and carefully planned wines with appropriate food.

☐ that the company should be like-minded, otherwise the whole thing becomes a bit tedious and unbalanced; off-putting for expert and non-expert alike.

☐ that reasonable time be allowed for thinking about the wine. The host and hostess must time the service of wine and food to accommodate this. *Nothing* is more irritating and fatuous, in my opinion, than for a host to say 'what is it?' and then blurt out the answer in whole or in part before one has had a chance properly to examine the wine.

☐ that the length of time is *not* dragged out and that one is never forced to a complete and final answer if one is not naturally forthcoming. Indeed, in mixed (not just 'genders,' but professional and lay) company I think it probably tactless of the host to try to extract nearest answers in a competitive manner. If people *want* to be sporting, let them have a go. (This can be a good thing, for one is stimulated into thinking along fresh lines by hearing other people's reactions, and one finds perhaps a new point of view engendered.) It should be remembered on the other hand, that some people can no more guess wines in public than they can stand on a table and sing; their minds become blank as panic sets in!

The dinner party host has peculiarly difficult responsibilities. There is a danger of two extremes that can be disheartening and deadly, respectively. Disheartening if beautiful wines are produced and not noticed or commented on at all; deadly if too much of a rigmarole is made of the occasion. Even variations in the middle range can be unsatisfactory. It is little satisfaction for a wine-loving guest to enjoy the wine but not to know what it is. The very least that should be provided is a small menu card with the wines listed, to be taken away by the interested guest.

Quite frankly, I carry a little note card and make notes furtively or blatantly depending on how well I know the host.

Menu and wine cards

How does one provide a menu card without revealing in advance the names of the wines? There are at least two ways. One is to provide a small folded card with a seal. When the seal is broken, the list of wines is revealed inside. (I came across this recently, charmingly done, by that most articulate of wine lovers, Tony Alment, one of that excellent breed of civilized medical men who seem to be the universal backbone of wine-loving fraternities.) The other is a variation I now use, slightly more elaborate in that it reveals the identity of each wine in turn. I write the menu on the left hand side of a stiff card, and the matching list of wines, well spaced, on the right. Each wine name is covered with a finger of paper or card held in place by a paper clip. Those who aren't busily guessing, or who can't wait, can quietly remove the covers. Those who want to rise to the challenge and plug away until they have exhausted their memory banks, can do so without keeping everyone in suspense.

It is nice to be able to arrive, by deduction, at a district or vintage. But I believe the main benefit of not knowing the wine in advance, even at a dinner party, to be this powerful concentration of thought and appreciative judgment which is, for the professional, a good discipline and, for the amateur, a continual test of discernment.

Before leaving the world of tasting mystique and expertise, I would like to concentrate on two interesting facets of blind tasting.

First impressions

One is the subconscious, evocative, memory that enables a taster, presumably highly sensitive to smells and tastes, to reach a perfect, or at least remarkably accurate, 'answer' to a wine tasted blind. The value of first impressions is well known to tasters but its true significance is less well understood. As we have seen from the chapter on the physical aspects of tasting, the sense of smell, though often a cinderella in development, is primitive or primal, and has the power of recalling a total experience from the memory, seemingly without the intervention of intellect.

What is most frequently *not* comprehended is that if the memory-brain does not instinctively and immediately produce an intelligible reaction, the reliance on this for the wine in question must be abandoned, and conscious reasoning must begin.

Deduction by elimination

This second approach is totally opposite to the reflex action of the first impression; it requires the exercise of positive intellectual effort; the use of eyes, nose and palate to *deduce* the answer that the nerve cells and memory failed to conjure up at 'first go'. I personally, at this stage, try to detect the grape used, the regional characteristics and work out a rough age-bracket. Then, by the process of elimination, arrive backwards at the answer, or, at any rate, at an intelligent *approximation* of district and vintage, with a definite opinion of quality. All this takes time and patience. The results are rarely as spectacular as those produced by the evocative memory. Furthermore it may well bore the bystander, unless the reasoning is concise and thought out aloud to sustain interest. The next chapter deals in greater detail with these important methods and techniques.

No cheating!   The very last word on this subject is an appeal for honesty, tempered with consideration. Cheating and short cuts in the tasting game are self-defeating. The true taster puts his blinkers on, is honest with himself, and is not influenced and led astray by others. On the other hand, the pursuit of zealous tasting expertise should only be pursued in appropriate company, and then only with discretion; otherwise the whole thing becomes a bore.

IX: Appreciation, recognition and deduction

The palate, like the eye, the ear, or touch, acquires with practice various degrees of sensitiveness that would be incredible were it not a well ascertained fact. T. G. SHAW, The Wine, the Vine and the Cellar, 1863

Having covered first principles, the senses, the approach to tasting and, broadly, those elements which give rise to taste, the time has come to dig a little deeper.

Tasting is not just an isolated theoretical exercise; it is usually an assessment of physical attributes in relation to a particular wine or wines, with some specific end in view (see page 7).

Purpose

It may well have one of the following purposes:
□ to assess the quality, state of development and possibly the value of a *known* wine,
□ to assess the relative quality and value of a known type of wine – possibly one of a range of similar or even identically-named wines,
□ to identify, from its physical taste characteristics, the style, region, quality and maturity of an *unknown* wine.

Basic problems

We might even reduce the taster's problems to a basic two:
□ knowing the name and full details of the wine, to judge its true qualities, etc., etc. This boils down to *appreciation* and *assessment*,
□ knowing little or nothing about the wine, to find *what* it is, from an accurate assessment of its characteristics, by tasting alone. This is encompassed by two words: *recognition* and *deduction*.

Context

Before embarking, however, I must stress that what follows must be seen in the context of a relaxed and informal group of like-minded 'amateurs' concentrating their attentions upon the merits of vintage wines. I am not writing about clinical laboratory tests to measure tasting thresholds, to isolate elements, to detect and quantify small differences in new wines made from experimental vines: these worthy endeavours we can leave to viticultural schools and oenological colleges. Equally out of court are those formally – and often excellently – organized tasting competitions, inter-district and international, where judges sit in splendid isolation to award medals to the best commercial entries. I am not trying to belittle either approach, though I confess I am confused and bored with much of the scientific approach to sensory evaluation, with its seeming emphasis on triangular tests, methodology, random numbers and abstruse mathematical formulae; and awarding gold medals can often be somewhat political, at best like beauty contests, when it appears to the interested onlooker that most of the really lovely girls have stayed at home. The fact of the matter is that really fine and great wines don't generally crop up in these circumstances, and if they did they would probably be wasted in such company.

Appreciation and assessment

Hedonistic approach

At its most elementary level, appreciation manifests itself in a positive liking (or not liking) for a wine, whether at a tasting or at a dinner party. At the same level, discrimination is expressed by a preference for one wine amongst a group of wines.

Wine merchants often find that even people fairly new to wine can be quite discriminating. Given two or three wines to taste, the customer will often express a marked preference for the best quality wine of a group, price notwithstanding. However, the layman falters in trying to express the *degree* of quality, and in sifting and describing the individual characteristics which, in combination, have awakened his natural taste instincts.

Relative quality

Without wishing to be condescending, what I am trying to say is that appreciation and simple discrimination are relatively easy. The next stage, assessment, is more complex and requires some background knowledge and tasting experience. Take one very important element, quality, for example. Quality is always relative. Even the best Jugoslav *riesling* will be on a lower quality plane than a good classic Rheingau such as a Rauenthaler Wieshell Riesling Spätlese; the best sparkling Loire wine rates lower than a good *grande marque* champagne like Bollinger; and the best unblended Beaujolais is below the peak of a good Côte de Nuits, such as a genuine Chambolle-Musigny from a reputable grower.

One has to know the relative quality planes before one begins.

Background knowledge

There is a whole kaleidoscope of tastes (and smells) that emanate from the physical characteristics of grape varieties, soil and climatic influences, wine-making techniques and the effects of age (see Chapter VI). They reveal style, areas, maturity as well as quality. The greater one's understanding of all these factors, the more accurate and rapid will be one's assessment and final pronouncement.

Recognition and deduction

We are now in the position where we are faced with a glass containing an unknown wine. The steps which follow – the processes of recognition and deduction – are perhaps the most difficult a taster ever has to contend with. He will have to bring to bear *all* his critical tasting faculties and knowledge.

Guessing?

Guessing is not allowed. Or is it? Let's not be too dogmatic, for there is surely only a fine dividing line between the inspired guess and split-second recognition: both may stem from a subconscious signal from the evocative memory.

However, what usually happens is that we are baffled by a half-familiar smell or taste that evades recognition. It remains 'on the tip of the tongue,' literally in this case, and the harder we try, the less is revealed.

If there *is* failure of recognition at this stage, the only solution is to 'back out' and attempt deduction by a systematic examination of taste characteristics. This needs not just a good palate *and* a detailed knowledge of regions and vintages, but the ability to link the reactions of the former with the recollections of the latter. This is, unhappily, as difficult as it sounds. There are, however, two useful techniques to bring to bear: elimination and bracketing.

Deduction by elimination

The technique of elimination entails a mental exercise. Take the most positively identified characteristics of the wine, compare them with the known characteristics of other wines, and cross off those that do not remotely match up. In other words, first eliminate all the obvious things it *cannot* be; then examine the things it *could* be; finally deduce what it *must* be. This simple and effective technique can be used to arrive at the grape variety, style and geographical area; even the district and vineyard. The method is also useful to confirm or strengthen opinions previously half-held.

'Classic' or 'foreign'?

What happens in practice is this: one picks up the glass of unknown wine and examines first its appearance, bouquet and flavour, sifting the normal, straightforward or 'classic' from the unusual or 'foreign.'

Take its appearance first of all. Is it unusually deep (this applies to either red or white) or abnormally pale (red mainly)? Is it strikingly young and purple, or 'sear and yellow'? Is it star bright or murky or slightly *pétillant*? The important thing is not just to notice these factors but to work out what might originate them. For example, unusual depth of colour in a red wine might be due to a fine hot vintage year in a temperate area like Bordeaux, or might indicate its origin in a sun-baked section of the Rhône valley, or from a normally hot region like the irrigated areas of South Australia. It could also arise from the vinification – a long fermentation which extracts a good deal of colour from the skins. With unusually pale-coloured wines the reverse might be true. All these will be clues, pointers. It is vital in the early stages *not* to jump to conclusions, but to leave the tracks open, passing on to the bouquet and then to the taste for a further crystallization of impressions, and then on to the final confirmation.

So, I repeat, get as many clues and leads from the appearance as possible; leave doubts hanging in the air and then pass on to the bouquet.

Marked characteristics

Once again one looks for any unusual or outstanding characteristics. First of all, whether there is a strongly marked grape aroma and whether it is from a classic region or not. If it *is* marked, and you recognize the grape, the areas where this grape is never grown can be eliminated. Incidentally, strength of bouquet, in the sense of fullness and forthcomingness is not the sole criterion, for a fine classic grape aroma can be light, even faint, particularly when the wine is young and undeveloped. What one is really looking for is clarity and purity. The more indeterminate, 'muddy' and neutral the smell, the poorer the quality of wine.

The most important thing of all is to realize that the combination of appearance and nose can provide many if not most of the clues to a wine's identity. By spotting the main characteristics of each and eliminating all that the wine *cannot* be, one then gains a clear idea confirmed by the palate; or one is left with likely alternatives that remain for the palate finally to sort out and decide.

Confirmation

In what way can the palate aid and confirm? First of all, consider the major taste factors which are noted on the palate: sweetness (in white wine, mainly), the degree of tannin, acidity, and alcohol; the extract; the continuity of grape characteristics (i.e. flavour to match the grape aroma); *finesse*, breed and, above all, length and intensity of flavour and finish – in short, quality. It is the linking of these taste factors to the colour and smell which should firmly anchor the total impression and lead one straight, or more safely by elimination, to a logical conclusion.

It will be obvious now, if it wasn't before, that one can only eliminate on a broad 'taste front' by having a wide knowledge to match; on a narrow front by having a detailed knowledge. Take heart, for though tasting experience is desirable, it is surprising how much can be achieved by limited experience aided by some theoretical knowlege of grape, district and age characteristics. By constantly reading wine books and articles one can, over a period, gain knowledge of what certain types of wine should taste like, and link the recollection of these characteristics to the actual taste of the wine in the glass. Indeed, I shall go one stage further and say that it is perfectly possible to deduce what a wine is even though one has never tasted this particular wine, or its type, before, simply by recognizing taste characteristics one has read or heard about. It would be rash for the taster in such circumstances to say that the wine *is* from such and such a vineyard; better to conclude that it *might well be*. Indeed, to be dogmatic at all in the field of tasting is both dangerous and tiresome.

What to expect

Now one of the difficulties facing the keen wine lover is finding out what a wine *should* taste like. By no means all of the many otherwise excellent books on wine actually help here. Nevertheless, if you read widely, an impression of the characteristics of the wines of various areas and districts will eventually be conveyed. A combination of reading, and visits (with tastings, of course) to wine areas is the best way of learning the salient characteristics. Chapter VII should point the student in the right direction.

Over a period of time, one's memory will be usefully stored with a battery of names and tastes – together with the inevitable exceptions to the rules that ensure that one never has a dull moment!

Deduction by bracketing

To round off the 'technique' section, here is a short exposition upon the useful method of bracketing, followed by two examples of blind tasting techniques in practice. The 'bracketing' technique also involves elimination. It is particularly useful when trying to assess the age of a wine.

Vintage deduction

Once again, some knowledge is required, this time of the vintage characteristics of the area one assumes, or knows, the wine to have come from. At one end of the bracket will be the *oldest* vintage it could possibly be;

at the other the *youngest*. The bracket may extend over ten or twenty years, or even a longer period in the case of really old wines.

The next stage is to fill in the most appropriate intervening vintages, eliminating the 'off-years' if the wine is robust, well made and 'classic' (and vice versa if the wine is light) until one is left with three or four possible vintage years. The final piece of elimination follows a thoughtful examination of the wine, comparing it against the known features of those singled-out vintages until, hopefully, one is left with just one inevitable choice of year. Incidentally, it is not sufficient merely to know that 1959, for example, was a big classic year in Bordeaux. It must also be borne in mind that not all the wines of the Bordelais are made in the same way, and that the types of grapes grown and blended can have different effects on the colour, bouquet and taste. One must know how the wines – at any rate the key wines – have developed in different districts, and be aware of the fact that the wines of St.-Emilion, for example, and certain red Graves, develop more quickly than the firmer wines of the Médoc. Once again, this sort of information is 'bracketed' in one's mind, and a conclusion often reached by the process of elimination described.

Examples

The trouble about trying to explain in words techniques that are second nature to the experienced taster is that the whole exercise is made to sound impossibly difficult. This is certainly not the intention. There is nothing I dislike more than the professorial use of long words where short ones would do, as if one had to surround oneself with an off-putting protective layer of super-professionalism. My aim all along has been to try and break down the barriers of the unknown into logical and progressive steps. If words are used that sound curious and stultified (or even pure 'winemanship') to the layman, let him remember that every specialist has his own peculiar vocabulary, whether he be a musician, lawyer or judge of dogs at Cruft's.

To help explain how elimination techniques work in practice, here are two examples of wines tasted blind at a 1970* Master of Wine study course. They were in a range of five unknown white and four unknown red wines.

The approach and notes made were precisely in this order:

'Wine No. 1' (red) APPEARANCE Unusually deep, indicating hot vintage conditions, either naturally or of an abnormally hot summer and early autumn. In other words, from South Australia; or a big classic Bordeaux of a particularly good year, or from the Rhône Valley. Just conceivably North African.

Actual colour a normal shade of red but with a marked purple edge to it, indicating immaturity.

A noticeably heavy bead ('legs') indicating high extract and glycerine. If, as is likely, the wine is from France, the combination of depth of colour and immature purple rules out recent poor vintages like '68 and

*As the same principles still apply, I do not see much is gained by up-dating these examples.

[68]

'65. It is unlikely to be '67; more likely '66 and just possibly '64 if from the Médoc.

BOUQUET 'Classic' and not 'foreign.' This rules out Australia, which often has a peculiar earthiness and 'hot' burnt smell. The grape aroma, however, is not easy to identify; certainly not *cabernet*, *pinot* or *gamay*, which rules out Bordeaux, and Burgundy north and south.

It smells 'sweet,' slightly scented, and certainly a heavyweight – the presence of considerable alcohol can be detected. Although young-looking, there is an absence of raw, youthful, mouth-watering acidity on the nose.

By virtue of elimination, and the combination of great weight and lack of the usual raw acidity, one turns to Rhône or possibly North Africa.

PALATE Very slight sweetness for a red (i.e. not austerely dry like many a Médoc). As full-bodied as it looks: heavy in the mouth, revealing considerable weight of alcohol, and full of extract. Robust yet curiously soft (lacking the excess tannin and acidity of a Bordeaux of the same weight and youthfulness). A nice, slightly scented flavour; still a little raw, and with a faintly bitter finish.

CONCLUSIONS A full-bodied, almost old-fashioned, Rhône wine from the south, around Châteauneuf. Good quality in its way; from an individual *domaine*, and of a recent big vintage, probably 1966. (The wine was, in fact, Clos du Mont Olivet 1966. Estate-bottled: Reflets du Châteauneuf-du-Pape. Alcoholic content over 14° G.L.)

'Wine No. 2'
(white)

APPEARANCE Noticeably deeper than the other whites in the range. Deep, old gold. Not very bright.

Distinctly an odd-man-out. From depth of colour could be a sweet dessert table wine or from some lesser region – perhaps Spain or South Italy. Could be due to excessive age in cask or bottle.

BOUQUET Rich, honeyed. Clearly a dessert wine and although not very distinct, sufficiently 'classic' to rule out Spain, Italy, etc. The honeyed overtones and richness would suggest *pourriture noble*, maturity and bottle age. Probably a sweet Bordeaux, or just possibly a sweet Loire like Coteaux du Layon.

PALATE The sweetness confirmed: in fact a medium-sweet dessert wine. Medium-full bodied. Certainly Sauternes (a sweet Loire would have had more acidity and less body). Not of first-growth quality but better than an ordinary 'sauternes supérieur'.

Clean, straightforward, but with a rather short flavour which rules out top quality. Balance quite good, indicating a soundly-made wine of a fairly reasonable vintage with some maturity.

CONCLUSIONS A heavy Barsac or medium Sauternes of *bourgeois* quality, 1962 or 1964 vintage.
(The wine was Château Pajot 1964, London-bottled.)

The ultimate
test

After all this palaver, it need hardly be added that tasting blind – recognizing a wine's precise origin and age by pure deduction – is the most severe test of true knowledge and ability.

Happily, however, it is not necessary to strive to reach, let alone to have reached, this stage of vinous euphoria in order to appreciate the taste of wine, and to enjoy drinking it. But if achievement in the higher realms of wine tasting *is* sought, it will now be apparent that a sensitive and trained palate alone is not enough. It has to be supported by real knowledge – of areas and districts, of grape varieties, of styles and methods, and of vintage characteristics. And a good technique is helpful.

X: How to organize a tasting

The buyer is recommended by Florentinus (Geoponica vii 7) to taste the wines he proposes to purchase, during a north wind, when he will have the fairest chance of forming an accurate judgement of their qualities.
HENDERSON, A History of Ancient & Modern Wines, 1824

Experienced wine shippers and merchants know perfectly well how to run their own tastings. The aim of this chapter is to advise younger members of the wine trade, amateur wine societies and tasting groups, what preparations are necessary and what pitfalls to avoid.

It is assumed that the purpose of any such tasting is to present a range of wines in the most favourable light either to induce sales, or simply to learn more about wine.

The first thing is to decide what type of tasting it is to be, what and how many wines are to be shown, and how many people are to participate. Very often, consideration of the latter point will dictate the number of wines and almost certainly the type of tasting, so this factor will be dealt with first.

How many tasters? Generally speaking, the seriousness and the effectiveness of a tasting is inversely proportionate to the number who attend. A large 'propaganda' tasting, attended by anything from sixty to three hundred people, will require a large hall or cellar, a large staff and very careful organization. The consumption, per capita, is bound to be greater than at a small tasting; and even if, as is wise, the range of wines is strictly limited, the expense may be out of all proportion to the ultimate benefit.

Forty to seventy guests may be considered the maximum manageable number at a standard stand-up and free-roaming tasting; half that number if a lecture/tasting is envisaged.

The aim of the tasting If the tasting is planned to launch a new branded wine, it ought really to be limited to this alone. Rather like the press review of a new model at the Motor Show, the aim will be to demonstrate the wine's desirable selling points, its drinkability, its price, the weight of supporting advertising and the attractions of the point-of-sale material. The gathering will generally be confined to salesmen, their customers, and members of the press, who will be expected to extol the product's virtues. Frankly, this is hardly a tasting in the wine lover's sense, but is not an infrequent type in these days of sophisticated wine marketing.

More traditional are the tastings organized by the wine shipper or merchant for his customers, presenting a range of wines of a new vintage or his current seasonal stock-in-trade. These are vital and informative tastings, that benefit both trade and consumer alike. Their proper organization is vital and the principles involved are discussed below.

Wine society or informal group tastings, usually aimed at the education and enlightenment of the members, who share the cost, can be similar in style to trade tastings, and most of the same problems arise.

But if the object is to *learn* something about wine, then by far the best type of tasting is the controlled and seated variety in lecture form, with carefully-selected wines used as illustrations. An occasion of this type will stand or fall on the knowledge and ability of the lecturer, and is usually best handled by a professional. One financial virtue of this type of tasting is that it is the most economical in terms of the amount of wine consumed.

How many wines?

At a big trade tasting there may well be from thirty to over one hundred different wines on show. It goes without saying that when there is a vast number of samples, the host expects his guests to discriminate, and also to spit out. After all, a trade buyer will only be in the market for wines of a certain type and price, and he won't waste his time, and cloud his mind, by tasting wines right out of the range of his own requirements.

The minute the public is let in, however, discrimination often goes by the board. Whereas the wiser and more experienced lay tasters will concentrate on those wines that interest them most, others will treat the whole thing as a sort of cocktail party and try to drink round the room, in the long run, wasting their time and the merchant's money.

It is far wiser for the organisers to be selective and to show only a limited range of say ten to twenty wines, outstanding representatives of their type and for price, even fewer if they are fortified wines i.e. port, sherry, etc. However, if the types are mixed, do make sure they are grouped clearly and that they are tasted in the right order, heavy sweet wines last.

Horizontal and vertical tastings

For a small club tasting or a lecture-tasting, then six to ten different wines will usually be enough. They must be well chosen, however, and worthy of study in depth. The most useful are 'horizontal' and 'vertical' tastings. Horizontal tastings are wines from different *châteaux* or different districts but all of the same vintage; vertical tastings compare different vintages of the same wine i.e. of the same *châteaux*, or of the same type or district. I have successfully combined a horizontal and vertical tasting on several occasions, with the same vintage of six different *châteaux* and six different vintages of one of those *châteaux*. The point of all this is not to make life complicated for the sake of complexity, but through the comparisons to learn more.

How much wine?

For drinking one allows approximately six to eight glasses per bottle, depending on the size of the glasses. For *tasting*, the number of glasses per bottle doubles, even trebles.

Allowing twelve to fifteen tasting glasses per bottle, the next thing is to estimate the number one should allow per person. At a controlled lecture-tasting the answer is quite simple, one per person. At a *serious* tasting where there is a big range of wines on show one can plan for a fairly small consumption on the basis that most tasters will try and taste a little of most of the wines on show. One should make allowances for the more popular types of wine, however, and provide adequate supporting stock.

However large or small the *range* of wines on show, one thing can be banked on: the bigger the crowd, the more per capita will be consumed. The hour of the day and duration of the tasting will also have a bearing.

Summing up: with a large range of wines and a small number of tasters, allow one bottle to six or seven people; for a small range and large crowd, one bottle may serve only three or four people. If it is just a casual tasting party, allow at least half-a-bottle a head. But with a smallish number of people at a tutored tasting, one bottle will serve fifteen or more tasters.

What time of day?

This short section deals with tastings that are business or social events, and not with internal staff tastings or visits to *chais*. The organizer has to bear in mind not only the appropriate times to taste, from the freshness of palate point of view, but the convenience of his guests. Indeed, the latter is usually of paramount importance.

It is the opinion of the writer that no serious tasting can be conducted during the course of a meal,* or, for different reasons (expounded in an earlier chapter) immediately after one. This leaves two practical alternatives: before lunch or early evening.

Duration

The timing of an evening function will depend a great deal upon social conventions. The main thing to remember when planning the programme is to leave ample time for the tasting. Twenty minutes or half-an-hour is simply not enough. Half-an-hour *may* be if the 'tasting' merely consists of a glass of something prior to a meal, for it then merely comes into the '7 for 7-30' category of invitation.

The length of time allowed for the tasting must be proportional to the number of wines on show and the number of guests invited. For ten to twenty wines and thirty to fifty people the time allowed should be somewhere between one-and-a-half and two hours. The point is, that although one solid hour of tasting is more than enough for even the hardiest taster, sufficient allowance has to be made for late-comers, early leavers and social chit-chat.

A controlled lecture-tasting is probably best held in the evening. The length of time required will depend partly upon the speaker. Two hours just sitting, sipping and listening is the absolute maximum. On the other hand, it is surprising how long it can take to taste and talk about only half-a-dozen wines. One should aim at about one-and-a-quarter to one-and-a-half hours. Incidentally, it is most important that everyone arrives on time, so invitations should be explicit: 7 for 7.15 prompt, or words to this effect.

Licensing laws

This section, of necessity, must confine itself to the British Isles, the licensing laws of which are complex enough without having to go further afield. Curiously enough, the English licensing laws are surprisingly inexplicit on the subject of tastings.

The moment that money changes hands or that licensed premises are used in connection with tastings, the laws of the land must be observed.

---

*Since originally penning this pontifical statement I have been privileged to attend a quite remarkable series of dinner tastings organized by Joseph Berkmann, one of London's most knowledgeable and enterprising restaurateurs. It surprised me how effective as well as interesting tasting a large range at table could be.

First of all, it is illegal for *any* person in an unlicensed situation (in the sense that although there are licence-*holders* it is *premises* that are licensed to sell wines, etc.) to sell wine by the bottle or glass. Strictly speaking, you cannot sell a bottle from your own private cellar to a friend without breaking the law. Bottles can only be sold from licensed premises, either fully licensed or 'off'-licensed. If an off-licence only is held, it is illegal for customers to pay for tasting samples, either by way of an entrance fee or per glass or per bottle if those samples are tasted on the premises.* Most wine merchants are in this position, but there is nothing wrong in him offering free samples for tasting, except in Scotland, where this is regarded, not illogically, as an inducement to make an eventual sale, something frowned upon by strong teetotal elements in certain licensing areas.

Only in 'on'-licensed premises (public houses, hotels and such-like – 'table' licences excluded) can tasting samples be sold by glass or bottle for consumption (which includes tasting and spitting-out) there and then.

Tasters under the age of eighteen are not permitted to consume wine on licensed premises, though there are no restrictions elsewhere.

Curiously enough, unlicensed amateurs are not so circumscribed. They can happily organize tastings at home, or in any other un-licensed premises, whether costs are shared on an *ad hoc* basis, or by subscription, or by the bottle-party method. What they must remember, however, is not to *sell* wine to each other or to non-members of a tasting group – even for charity. The organizers of big 'charity' tastings might be advised to clear their position with the police or local magistrate's court beforehand.

A wine merchant or his representative can also hold a tasting of his stock-in-trade on unlicensed premises too, so long as he makes no charge for entry or sale by the glass. He can also solicit orders at such a tasting so long as the orders are effected, i.e. the wines delivered, from 'off'-licensed premises.

To the organizers of private tastings my advice is, if in doubt say nothing; get on with it. A cautious official, not quite sure of laws of the land, may play safe at your expense. But if money changes hands, beware.

Organization of tastings

Big trade tastings are usually organized in suitable premises (in firms' cellars, even in the town hall) by experienced professionals, so we will confine our attentions to two moderate-sized types of tasting.

A tasting for twenty to sixty guests

Space and flow

Ideally, the organizer removes everything that will interfere with his table layout and customer-flow. At all costs clutter must be avoided; there will be little enough room for his own assistants and impedimenta. Crowds bring their own problems and one of the first, too often over-looked, is hats, coats and bags. If there is not a cloakroom or spare room nearby, then set aside a large table for coats, etc.

The most important considerations after this are spatial: there must be enough room for tasters to circulate without obstruction; there must be

*Though I believe that a bona-fide tasting club can charge for these events.

enough space between the different wines to allow tasters adequate elbow room; and also enough space, preferably barred to tasters, for staff and assistants to service the tasting tables.

Table layout

The key to success is table layout. This will depend on the shape of the room, but basically there are two approaches: to have a series of tables round the room (continuous or spaced) with the tasters circulating in the middle, or to have a 'square' of tables in the centre, enclosing staff and stock. The virtues of the latter are that fewer assistants are needed to supervise the tasting – opening bottles, keeping them in order, removing empty bottles and used glasses – and that the service and stock areas are safely isolated. On the other hand, assistants have to push through tasters to get to the central reservation. If a large number of wines are on display it is probably better to arrange the tables around the perimeter of the room. (Avoid corners, however, as these become congested.) They can be spaced better, and tasters can move from one area to another more easily. On the other hand, staff must be stationed at *each* table section. At a big tasting this will mean one assistant per six- or ten-foot section or per six wines.

Space requirements are often underestimated, particularly the space between different wines. Apart from the discomfort caused by nudgers, wines get mixed up and out of order if arranged too closely. To avoid this, allow only four to six bottles to a ten-foot (three-metre) trestle table, depending on the number of tasters expected. The more tasters, the wider the spacing.

Sequence

The wines should be laid out in the correct order of tasting and, most important and not always easy, incoming guests must be made aware of the sequence of wines and encouraged to taste in that order. This is where a clearly laid-out tasting list comes in handy: the list and table layout should coincide. One very important point: do not place table Number One too near the entrance as a queue of early tasters may form and impede the passage of other guests and assistants. If the room is small it is often desirable to start the tasting on the far side to avoid congestion. If there are sweet or fortified wines on show at a mixed tasting it is essential to discourage guests from tasting them first, so place them at the end of the natural tasting sequence and traffic flow.

Side tables

Still on the subject of layout, and ignoring for the moment decoration and other incidentals, it is better to have quite separate tables for glasses, literature and food. Ideally, the table for glasses and tasting cards should be placed somewhere between the entrance and the first wine to be tasted. Literature of the take-home variety should be handed out from a table by the exit. No purpose is served by burdening guests with reading matter at the start or in the middle of the tasting. It won't be read during the tasting and the odds are that it will be discarded before the tasting is over.

Placing of spittoons

Spittoons are not easy to place. They should not be on the tasting tables but on the floor, either just in front of the tables (if the wines are well spaced and there is ample room for tasters' feet) *or* sufficiently away from the tables not to trip people up. They are probably best placed six or eight feet away from the tables, more if crowds are expected, to allow an appropriate width of passage for circulation and to encourage tasters to retreat from the table with their tasting samples, allowing other tasters a chance to get to the tables. There is nothing more irritating at a tasting than a 'clinging vine' who stations himself semi-permanently by a bottle, helping himself, making notes (one hopes) and spitting, all without moving his feet. An out-of-reach spittoon helps to discourage this.

The 'tutored tasting'

The room size required must be directly related to the numbers attending, for each taster, as well as the lecturer, will need a chair *and* table space.

Tables essential

Make no mistake about it, tables are vital. It is impossible to conduct this sort of tasting session with tasting cards, pencils – possibly maps and other literature – and glasses, on one's lap.

Either individual small tables or desks should be used, allocating one per taster. Larger tables may, of course, be shared. In any event, the spacing per person must be wider than a row of closely adjacent chairs. Allow at least a metre so that there is room on each section of table for several glasses in a row, and for notes.

It is much more comfortable for all tasters to face the lecturer, so only one side of the table should be used. If the tables are in continuous rows then there must be sufficient space between those rows for the people to pass along to serve the wines. It is a mistake to assume that fewer assistants are required for lecture-tastings, for although there may be just one lecturer, the timing of the service of the wines is very important and sufficient serving staff or willing helpers must be laid on.

Wine service

There are two ways of serving the wine: pouring it out at table, or, alternatively, in another room, or at the back of the hall, if it can be done without distraction (popping corks are usually accompanied by loud cheers!), bringing it in on trays. Assuming that a tasting quantity may range from about ten to fifteen glasses per bottle, it is desirable to have one assistant per bottle, i.e. per ten to fifteen tasters, otherwise the time taken pouring is apt to disturb the lecturer and fragment the session. It is difficult for tasters to concentrate whilst assistants are moving around with the wine, and if the service is protracted there is always the danger that those who get the wine first will be tempted to taste the wine 'solo' instead of waiting to be guided through the mysteries of colour, bouquet and flavour by the lecturer.

The problem of spittoons is even more acute with a seated audience. They should be behind the chairs, one between two tasters being ideal. Alternatively, small plastic cups can be placed on the table before each taster. On the other hand, with a restricted number of wines at such a seminar, the wine can be swallowed.

Details to bear in mind

Tables

It may seem silly to say this, but the essential thing is that tables should be of normal dinner-table height, and firm. In other words, don't use tiny coffee tables or flimsy, rocking trestle tables. Nor should the tables used be too high or too wide, as they can be difficult to serve across.

Table coverings

Several factors should be borne in mind: red wine stains; bottles can scratch; and a white background is essential to show off the colour of the wine.

So, *cover* your table, whether it is plain deal or polished mahogany. If the latter, use a large white cloth with newspaper or some other lining underneath. If an ordinary trestle table is used, a white table cloth or rolls of plain white paper can be pinned to it.

Lighting

This is important, and yet often the least considered factor. Candles add appropriate glamour to the occasion *but*, truthfully, although a myriad of candles may *look* pretty they really don't produce enough of the sort of light in which the colour of wine can be seriously judged. Last, but not least, candles consume oxygen and will help to make a small room hot.

On the other hand, ordinary blue fluorescent lighting is disastrous. It gives red wine an unhealthy dark, blue-black tinge and will make it appear far younger and less mature than it really is.

Daylight is best; failing that, ordinary tungsten or warm-white fluorescent lighting.

Mind you, there is no reason why candles, either in proper candelabra or stuck in the top of empty bottles, shouldn't be used in conjunction with artificial light. One or two per table look attractive, and they are handy for observing the clarity of the wine.

Service or self-service?

At an ordinary, largish tasting, is it better for the hosts to pour out the wine, or should guests be allowed to help themselves? In practice, whatever is decided, there is usually a bit of both. At a well-attended tasting, the staff will be busy doing several jobs at once, serving the wines, drawing corks and clearing away abandoned glasses. It is fairly certain that they won't be able to spend all their time helping the guests to wine, even if this is supposed to be their main job.

On the other hand, if tasters help themselves too liberally at a free-for-all tasting, then a bit of judicious and tactful pouring will be called for. This will prevent the host's stocks being depleted too rapidly and will encourage guests to taste a wider range more effectively.

Assistants and staff

Do not under-estimate the number of people required to help, from chief to cloakroom attendant. Numbers and calibre of staff will, of course, depend on the nature of the event, its size and the place.

Small club tastings are usually no problem. Just make sure you have members prepared to lend a hand.

Many small- and medium-sized trade tastings will be manned by members of the firm, usually principals and sales staff who know their subject and are identifiable by lapel badges bearing their name and/or that of their company.

When tastings are held in catering establishments – hotels, restaurants or clubs – staff will generally be employed. Even if supervised by a head waiter or 'captain', it should never be assumed that they will know exactly what is required. So a cardinal rule is to *brief all staff before the tasting commences:* where to station themselves, how many bottles to open, how much to pour; to clear glasses and avoid clutter, etc.

Insist on rigorous stock control, with a complete complement of bottles, full or empty, after the tasting, otherwise bottles simply disappear. Another tip is to provide a supply of inexpensive wine or beer for the staff to wet their whistles on – for afterwards.

Let *one* person be in overall charge. Have enough 'front of house' personnel to host and advise; enough staff or assistants to serve. Don't forget to man the cloakroom and reception table(s). Make sure *everyone* knows precisely what he or she is to do.

Spittoons, bottles and funnels

Properly equipped tasting rooms have permanent spittoons of a basin, fountain or flushing variety.

At the sort of tastings we have just been discussing, however, mobile spittoons are the order of the day and they run to three types: the pedestal funnel variety, rather like a fat version of one of the nastier types of road-house ash-tray; the sawdust box or bucket; and the table-top bowl or cup. The very best resemble old-fashioned barber's shaving pots and are now rare collectors' pieces.

Quite the simplest to prepare and satisfactory to use is the sawdust box. This type of spittoon is just a wooden wine case with the top removed and the inside two-thirds filled with sawdust. It is commodious and fairly absorbent; to be on the safe side, line it with oil-cloth or polythene. Unhappily, it is easy to trip over a box in a crowded room.

If you can't find enough boxes, buckets of sand or sawdust will do. They present a smaller target, however, and knock over more easily. Incidentally, empty bottles, with glass or plastic funnels stuck in the neck, seen on tables at many trade tastings, are *not* spittoons. They are receptacles for the taster to empty his glass in before moving to the next wine. One often wonders about what happens to all the secondhand but almost virginal wine which is accumulated (staff perks? cooking wine? or re-corked as Château Grande-Mélange?)

Glasses

Stemmed glasses of a standard bowl shape are best. Naturally, at a large tasting, quantity and not quality of glassware must prevail. Standard stemmed varieties are perfectly adequate and can be hired at a reasonable price from any reputable catering firm. The six-ounce size tends to be too big for a tasting. Five-ounce glasses may be found more suitable, or even, at a pinch, large port glasses. Other suitable types are sherry *copitas* and 'dock' glasses. The ideal tasting glass is illustrated on page 19.

The quantity of glasses required needs careful consideration. All depends on the number of different wines on show and the number of people expected. It is rarely a practical proposition to provide one glass per person per wine. At a large tasting one glass is normally provided on arrival and the taster is expected to use it throughout the tasting, though a clean glass is usually obtainable if by chance the first is abandoned or if a fresh one is really required. If wines of contrasting colour and style are shown at the same tasting a change of glasses should be allowed for.

If the basis is one glass per taster, allowance must be made for 'wastage': breakages, abandoned glasses, etc., so order double the quantity first thought of.

Nothing looks worse than a litter of partially-filled glasses, particularly on tasting tables, so staff should continually remove them. If they are left on the tables they are confusing, get in the way and only encourage other people to leave theirs too.

If there are insufficient glasses, or if proper washing-up facilities are not available, it may be necessary to put rinsing bowls in the tasting room. They can look unsightly, however, and might be objected to on the grounds of hygiene. If assistants *are* expected to wash glasses on the spot, washing-up bowls should be either behind the table out of sight or on a rear service table.

How many bottles?

Even at a big and busy tasting it is better to have only *one* bottle of each wine open at a time. This is not just for the sake of economy; its main purpose is to avoid clutter and to prevent the bottles from getting out of order. It also discourages guests from picking up open bottles and wandering off with them, ostensibly to assist their friends. It usually stays with the group until it is consumed!

Nor should the entire tasting stock of bottles of each wine be put on the table in serried ranks. They may look impressive, but they soon get in the way of the serving staff. Bottles are picked up for a close look at the label – and usually put back in the wrong place, all of which adds to the disorganization and mess. However, it is not a bad idea to have one other bottle, opened but stoppered, on the table by the tasting bottle. It acts as an immediate reserve and enables waiting tasters to look at the label and the general presentation of the bottle. The point is, it is difficult to see the label of a wine being poured; it is usually obscured by hand or napkin. Last, but not least, the number of wines open for tasting may be dictated by the heat of the room. A cold white wine can gain ten degrees (F.) in as many minutes.

Corks and capsules

The presentation of sample bottles is important. The capsules should be cut as for a dinner party, just below the top of the neck and the top removed. Do not remove the entire capsule. Next wipe the top of neck and cork with a damp cloth and finally with a clean dry cloth.

After removing the cork, preferably in one piece – not so easy with older wines – it should be tied to the neck, wine-side up, with an india-rubber band. Lastly a wedge-shaped stopper cork is inserted until it is time to serve.

Older wines should of course be decanted. Make sure the decanter is identified by name or number. The empty bottle should be kept alongside, with cork, for inspection.

Food?

Except at press receptions and the more social type of tasting, food should be kept to a minimum. It merely distracts and provides counter-flavours and smells.

Nevertheless, it must be accepted that some people need something to cleanse their palates between wines. Cheese squares and dry biscuits are the conventional answer to this problem; dry bread and plain cold, but not iced, water are alternatives.

It is perhaps important also to bear in mind that virtually all red wines and most whites have been devised by nature and man as an accompaniment for food. In fact, wine tastes *different* with food, and if to be

[79]

pre-judged in a food context it is often easier to do so at a tasting with a nibble of something appropriate.

The old saying 'buy a wine over apples and sell it over cheese' has much more than a grain of truth in it. Cheese makes wine taste softer, mellower and sweeter. The riper and more 'smelly' cheeses are better with rougher reds; they tend to overpower a delicate flavoursome wine. An over-ripe brie, for example, will kill a mature burgundy stone dead. The other dangers of the richer and more exotic cheeses are that the smell will compete with the bouquet of the wine and can create in a warm tasting room a decidedly unpleasant atmosphere.

So, safe and satisfactory are small squares of a mild cheese of the cheddar variety. One generous plateful per tasting table, with tooth-picks for those too delicate to use their fingers.

Reverting to apples for a moment, one English wine merchant, well-known for his port, used to clean his palate with a bite of apple between tasting samples of young vintage port. I confess I have not tried this method though sorely tempted. There are few wines more palate-numbing than immature vintage port.

No smoking – or strong scent

One would have thought that the 'no smoking' rule at tastings was sufficiently known and understood. But it seems that smokers are a law unto themselves; they do not even consider the spent matches and cigarette ends as litter, but unthinkingly discard them anywhere. A man who reaches automatically for his pipe and pouch at home or in the office will do so with equal unconcern when he has reached the contemplative end of a tasting.

So, beware. At a big public tasting put NO SMOKING signs up. Catch smokers politely at the door and advise all assistants to watch out for the tell-tale wreaths of blue smoke, particularly among the groups who are chatting in a relaxed fashion, their tasting completed.

Ladies should also refrain from using strong scent and powder. The delicate bouquet of wine simply cannot compete with a host of foreign smells. It is difficult enough to cope with the scent of wine without the nostrils being assaulted by smoke and perfume at the same time.

Tasting cards

There is no surer way of wasting one's efforts than to invite guests to taste without providing some form of 'score-card' – a pre-printed list, folder or tasting card – for them to consult, make comments on, and take away afterwards.

There are three essential requirements:

☐ The card should contain the full name and vintage of each wine, in tasting order, with the price against each if a trade tasting.

☐ There should be space for comments either alongside or underneath each wine or on a blank page opposite. *At least* as much space should be allowed for comment as the name of the wine occupies. It is surprising how often no room is left at all.

☐ It should be printed on card or stiff paper. Flimsy paper is hopeless to write on while standing up, and crumples easily when filed.

Embellishments such as wine maps and descriptions of wine districts, etc., can be included. Occasionally price list and tasting card are combined. The scope for variety is immense; but whatever form it takes, a tasting card is basically only an *aide-mémoire;* for with wine, as with many other things, it is a matter of 'in at one ear and out of the other' unless specific action is taken to remedy the lazy human condition.

Summary

Plan the tasting well in advance. Consider all the vital factors: date, time, place; number of guests and assistants; the type and number of wines. Do not leave important details until the last minute. The check list on the following page may come in handy.

Check list for tastings

In advance
- ☐ Guest list
- ☐ Room booking
- ☐ Wine selection and stock reservation
- ☐ Printing: invitations, tasting cards
- ☐ Order tables, cloths, glasses and other sundries
- ☐ Forewarn assistants; book staff

Pre-tasting checks
- ☐ Cloakroom facilities
- ☐ Tasting room layout
- ☐ Tables – number, size, arrangement
- ☐ Table cloths or rolls of white paper
- ☐ Wine (delivered well in advance, to settle); temperature
- ☐ Two bottles of each wine at each tasting position; supporting stock
- ☐ Corkscrews: one per assistant or one per table (there are never enough)
- ☐ Stopper corks, wedge-shaped
- ☐ Elastic bands for securing original corks to bottle necks
- ☐ Lapel badges for hosts and assistants
- ☐ Glasses: right quantity, shape and size (polished *and* clean smelling)
- ☐ Tasting room lighting: correct intensity, type and position
- ☐ Spittoons or sawdust boxes
- ☐ Cloths or napkins for glasses and wiping bottle necks. One per assistant
- ☐ Empty bottles with glass or plastic funnels for dregs
- ☐ Candles, candelabra or empty bottles, and matches
- ☐ Rinsing bowls, if necessary
- ☐ Plain cheese cubes, and plates
- ☐ Dry biscuits, dry bread, and plates
- ☐ Jugs of water (without ice)
- ☐ Trays for removal of glasses
- ☐ Tasting cards or sheets
- ☐ Price lists, supporting literature, hand-outs
- ☐ Sharpened pencils or ball-point pens
- ☐ Maps and posters for decoration. Drawing pins and adhesive tape
- ☐ Visitors' book
- ☐ NO SMOKING signs (and hide all ash trays, to discourage smokers)
- ☐ Lock-up room for storage of wine overnight, if on strange premises

Staff, assistants
- ☐ Brief carefully before tasting commences
- ☐ Allocate 'stands', tables, duties
- ☐ Number of bottles to be opened, timing
- ☐ Keeping tables uncluttered, removal of empty glasses
- ☐ Boozers, free-loaders and smokers – refer to host/organizer

After the tasting
- ☐ Stock check
- ☐ Separation of unopened, opened and empty bottles*
- ☐ – and so to bed!

*For extra security, insist on all opened bottles to be replaced in their original cases. A full case will indicate that there has been no pilfering by staff.

XI: How to record tasting notes

. . . add a little to the literature of one of the three great joys in life.
GEORGE SAINTSBURY Notes on a Cellar-book, 1920

Why make notes?

Only two kinds of person can do without tasting notes: the rare and fortunate individual with a phenomenally freak memory, and the less rare type who chooses not to complicate matters by ever tasting more than the firm favourites he knows and likes. (There is, in fact a third: the really experienced specialist who spends every day tasting wines in his own particular field. For example, the sherry, port or whisky blender. His highly-developed palate for a comparatively limited range of smells and tastes may not require the support of the written word, save to record the names and proportions of the constituent parts selected for the blend.)

So, make notes. You will find them useful, and referring back to them enjoyable. Here are some methods:

Essential information

Frankly, any system is adequate that stores sufficient information for an individual's purpose in a speedy and accessible manner.

The following information is more or less essential:

☐ The date of tasting (too often omitted in the heat of the moment).
☐ The name of the wine (district, vineyard).
☐ The vintage year.
☐ If in bottle, the name of the bottler (if estate-bottled the name of the estate. Château-bottlings merely require the qualifying initials C.B.). If from the cask, 'ex cask.'
☐ The price (per bottle, per dozen or per hogshead, as appropriate).
☐ A description of the appearance of the wine: colour, depth, clarity.
☐ A description of its nose: aroma, bouquet.
☐ A description of its taste: component parts, finish.
☐ General conclusions: maturity, quality, value.

One important point should be made. Just because there are myriads of descriptive terms available it is not essential or desirable to overdo it; indeed, the experienced taster will tend to note only the outstanding and meaningful characteristics, and the *exceptions*.

A typical page of entries from my own notebook system is illustrated on the next page. In practice I add the names of the wines to a running index arranged by country and district. I also note the occasion, the host, the place. If it is a special dinner, the food. Frankly it is very much up to the individual.

Card system

Of the various methods of collating tasting notes the card system has many virtues. A separate card for each wine is stored in district, vintage or alphabetical order. This system is very handy for quick reference. Appropriate sections can be extracted and taken to the tasting room thus

Date	Wine	Year	Shipper etc.	Appearance	Bouquet	Palate; conclusions
3/7 73	Tasting at Chelsea Town Hall for Junior Branch of the International wine and Food Society					
*	Chiroubles	71	F.B. Jacques Dépannieux retail £1.39p	light in colour; youthful pink. attractive	very pleasant and forthcoming gamay aroma. clean & refreshing.	dry, light, agreeable fruity flavour and refreshing acidity. charming but a bit short on quality
	Pouilly Blanc Fumé M. du Nozet	70	F.B. Ladoucette £2.25	pale; straw-tinged; very bright.	pronounced aroma; black-currant sauvignon over-mouth-watering	Very dry; lightish. Thin but flavoury. Verging on tart. Expensive
**	Gewürztraminer	70	F.B. Hugel £1.60	fuller in colour; more yellow.	lovely soft spicy aroma.	medium-dry, medium-full; fat and rich, yet delicate. Soft. agreeable. Nice wine
18/7	at the château. Hosts: Mr. & Mrs. Sam Pray					
**	Ch. Beychevelle	64	C.B.	fairly deep; still some immaturity	fine deep bouquet, developing well.	fairly full-bodied; becoming round and velvety. Fruity. Still plenty of tannin & acidity. A good '64.
23/7	Tasting of Hungarian Wines at Christie's for the Institute of Masters of Wine. Hosts Herr Dömötor and Fred May					
	Bull's Blood of Eger	67	London-bottled	fairly full plummy red	rather common stalky & peppery	fullish; soft though peppery. Ordinary.
*	Debroi Harslevelu	69	Bottled by F. & E. May	pale straw-yellow.	unfamiliar but attractive nose	medium-dry; medium-full. Typical soft Hungarian character. Nice wine
**X	Egri Leanyka	47	From the State cellars	medium-pale Gold-tinged. remarkably youthful-looking for its age	soft, rich, 'milky' bouquet. exquisite.	medium sweet, fullish for a white wine. Soft, lovely honeyed flavour. Excellent balance and finish. A most remarkable wine
1/8 **	Brunello di Montalcino	61	Estate-bottled By ondi-Santi	deep coloured garnett red heavy bead (legs) some maturity	incredibly deep, rich yet delicate and scented.	Dry; full-bodied—huge in fact. Rich fully-packed flavour. Fairly tough, almost roasted and with touch of iron in the finish.
4/9 **	Graham	1887	Original branded cork. Very mature	light in colour; tawny but with healthy glow	rich; complex; refined—but an old man, tiring	considerable sugar loss but still semi-sweet. Light but residue of fatness and body. lovely flavour ethereal and lingering.
8/9 **X	Bonnes-Mares	61	bottled by Army & Navy Stores	fine, rich medium-deep mature	magnificent pure ripe pinot aroma. very forthcoming.	slightly sweet as red wines go; medium-full; silky, rich, soft & beautifully balanced.
X *	Côte-Rôtie	66	F.B. Paul Jaboulet Aîné	deep, fine maturing.	most attractive and stylish. Fruity and immediately appealing	full-bodied but with lovely balance and excellent flavour. Rhone at its best. Keep longer.
2/11	Special pre-sale dinner at Christie's. Harry Waugh, Cyril Ray, Eddie Penning-Rowsell, Hugh Johnson et al.					
	Ch. Lafite 1870 en magnum from the cellars of Glamis Castle		Wax seal embossed Coningham wine. magnificent robe	incredibly deep and youthful for a century-old	rich, fruity, many layered. Not a trace of mustiness sourness or acidity	a fabulous experience; rich, full, velvety, complete. Perfect harmony & balance. So this is what pre-phylloxera wines were like!

saving considerable time as headings are already prepared and do not have to be re-written.

The main disadvantages are that it is a bulky system and individual cards can get misplaced or lost.

Tasting book

Notes are entered as the wines are tasted, in chronological order. The advantage of this system is that a series of pocket-sized books instead of boxes of cards can be used. The pages should be ruled up vertically to save endless writing of main headings.

The disadvantages are the amount of writing required (details of each wine have to be entered every time) and the need for an accurate and up-to-date index to make quick reference possible.

Ring binders

Another system shown to me recently combines the virtues of card and book. It consists of ruled up or printed leaves, arranged horizontally and set into a ring or spiral binder. It is used like a book but leaves can be inserted as and where necessary.

Loose-leaf

Like the card system, the wines can be kept in any order – district, vintage or alphabetical. (This combines the virtues of cards and books but tends to be bulky unless several wines can be written-up on one page.)

All methods require time, patience and an orderly mind (or an obliging secretary with these attributes). Like playing the piano – many start, few continue. Like piano-playing, it is worth the effort in the long run, unless, of course, one is tone deaf!

Competitive score cards

Wines submitted to a panel of judges for comparative and competitive tasting have to be tasted methodically. Almost invariably a pre-printed tasting card is supplied, indicating the factors to be noted and assessed and giving each factor, or each group, a numerical value.

Points are awarded for positive features; negative points for faults. Maximum possible can be 7 points, more often 20, sometimes 100.

The points 'weighting' depends on the type and class of wine to be tasted, and the purpose of the tasting. For commercial entries judges might be allowed up to 4 points for colour, 6 for bouquet, and 10 for taste; possibly 5, 5 and 10. There are more sophisticated and elaborate points systems, but the majority of readers will not come across them.

For fine wines I would recommend a relatively simple system:

	points
APPEARANCE (depth, hue, clarity, viscosity)	4
BOUQUET (condition, development, grape aroma, bouquet)	5
TASTE (dryness, body, tannin, acidity, balance)	6
OVERALL QUALITY (finesse, complexity, finish)	5
total possible score	20

Having decided on the type of tasting-note system, what descriptive words should one use? The following chapter should be of help.

XII: The use of words

The first difficulty that tasters encounter is to find and to translate into precise and clear language the qualities and defects of a wine . . .
PIERRE BRÉJOUX, Revue du Vin de France, 1977

The problem

Put quite bluntly, most people simply do not know how and where to start describing a wine, and many are reluctant even to express an opinion. Some, knowing more, are less shy; but do they really mean what they say, or is a familiar sounding wine word being used just because it *is* familiar sounding, perhaps impressive? The odds are that it will not convey the speaker's intention.

Renewed thoughts on the use of words in relation to wine were stimulated by an interesting paper by Adrienne Lehrer* which had been typically misquoted by a 'highbrow' Sunday newspaper and picked up, more accurately, by *Decanter* magazine. However, I was really jogged into action by contradictory statements about identical wines made by fellow Masters of Wine on a recent visit to the winelands of the Cape. It seemed to me that if untrained laymen in America *and* experienced English professionals could disagree on whether a wine was full or light or dry, or whatever, it was less likely to be a sensory problem than semantic: either carelessness in the use of words or alarming imprecision.

Clearly some guidance is needed.

Are words necessary?

It might justifiably be asked at this stage whether it is necessary to use words at all? Surely wine can be consumed, enjoyed, appreciated to the full without a word being said or written?

Why talk or write about wine?

There are several reasons for talking or writing about wine. Basically:
(i) to express a simple preference of one wine to another
(ii) to increase the awareness of other tasters
(iii) to communicate the style, quality, condition etc. of a wine to someone else.

On what sort of occasion?
– tastings

The context in which wine is tasted is all important. In Chapter II I mentioned different circumstances in which wine is tasted, from the cask to the table. On each one of these occasions a written or mental note would be made, possibly after discussion with the cellar-master or merchant, or whomsoever.

At the sort of tastings described in Chapter X one would normally make notes, ranging from an abbreviated preferential tick or cross to more detailed descriptions at a tutored tasting.

Talking about Wine in the journal *Language*, Volume 51, Number 4 (1975) by Adrienne Lehrer, Committee of Linguistics, College of Liberal Arts, University of Arizona.

– *lecturing*	A lecturer on wine has several responsibilities: (i) to stimulate interest and enthusiasm (ii) to 'open the eyes' of the audience by drawing attention to features they might not have noticed (iii) to select words which are evocative and meaningful (iv) to use words which can be clearly related to the wine being tasted by his audience (v) in the case of lecturing wine trade students within the trade, to guide them in the use of words, particularly those long-tried and conventional terms which, when written, will be understood by an examiner or, equally, by a customer.
– *selling wine*	It is fairly common practice for wine merchants to annotate their lists, describing the qualities of different types of wine, of vintages, even of individual wines. Similar eulogies will be conveyed by the salesman to the potential customer. It is much less difficult to use words in a selling context, possibly because the descriptions are qualitative and general, not analytical: pleasure-invoking adjectives, and opinions regarding readiness to drink, rather than specific descriptions. Also, in the case of white wines, whether sweet or dry; reds, whether full-bodied or light.
– *at dinner parties*	There are many reasons for giving, or attending, a dinner party. If it is mainly a social event, grand or less formal, the purpose will be to impress or to entertain: the occasion and the people will take precedence over the fare. The food and the wine are likely to be relegated to a supporting role. The choice of wine will depend on appropriateness and price. It is not provided as a subject for discussion. Even so, if you are keen on wine there is no harm in making a discreet note. However, if it is a food-and-wine occasion, the hostess and host will expect comments, even a discussion, though the level and intensity will depend as much on the people present as the quality of fare. The point is: whether wines are discussed with intensity or not at all will depend on the type of dinner, the people and the intention. To pontificate on wine in a non-wine context is tactless; not to comment intelligently on wine in a wine-orientated context is a mis-use of the occasion.

Great wine – for whom?

Arising out of my travels over the past few years it is abundantly clear that the vast majority of owners of fine and rare wines have a major concern; on what occasion, and for whom, shall their vinous treasures be opened? It is less a matter of money than sheer waste, and the knowledge that once a cork is drawn, that's it. A fine picture can be looked at scores of times, and re-sold; a piece of silver can be admired for its beauty of craftsmanship, and still has intrinsic value. Apart from *haut-cuisine*, great wine is the only work of art which has to be consumed in order to be appreciated. Thereafter its only value is a treasured memory.

It seems sensible therefore to keep the finest wines for dinner parties (or tastings) which will be attended by people who *know* about wine, or at the very least are like-minded convivial souls. Having gathered together fine wine and appreciative palates, host and guest alike are unlikely to be satisfied with grunts, nods and mere smacking of lips.

Choice of words	Fine wine demands to be talked about. Words are needed. There is a wide spectrum of words, but they more-or-less boil down into two categories: factual and fanciful. There is a place for both. It is frequently said that no speakers mean exactly the same thing by the same words, or that no word ever means the same thing twice!*
	When it comes to wine, 'facts' very often turn out to be opinions. Let's not be put off by academic pedants. Better to fumble and stumble than not to try at all.
Basic words	At the end of the chapter, just before the glossary, I have extracted a short list of words which, if carefully (I avoid the word 'correctly') used are meaningful to English tasters who have had a modicum of training and experience.
Fanciful words	By all means let us indulge in flights of poetic expression, similes, flower analogies and so forth, but be careful about the context.
Unqualified and ambiguous words	One taster will loosely described a wine as 'full', another taster might disagree totally. The point here is that 'full', unqualified, can conjure up several meanings in other tasters' minds: full-coloured (deep), full-bodied (high alcohol and extract), full bouquet (i.e. well developed, very forthcoming), full-flavoured (positive, mouth-filling).
	So adjectives like 'full' or 'light' should either be qualified or used in a distinctly recognisable context: colour, bouquet, weight-in-the-mouth, style, flavour, etc.
	Words such as 'hot' and 'round' can have several meanings. A list of ambiguous words appears on page 93.
Use of similes and analogies	The French themselves, in writing and in speech, tend to be far more poetic than the English, their descriptions often roaming up a romantic path, associating wine with the more delicate aspects of love-making and flowers, scents and exotic foods. The English are generally more reticent, more terse and, let's be honest, often less imaginative. I find I cannot generalise about Americans. Their writing and talking depend on so many factors, from ethnic background to type of reader and audience. There *is* a tendency, in some quarters, to verbosity and polysyllables, many Americans preferring to use long words rather than clear simple expressions, but this is not confined to those who write, or speak, about wine. One could argue that likening a bouquet to violets or saying a taste is reminscent of truffles is not very meaningful if the listener or reader is unfamiliar with the smell of one and the flavour of the other. Yet I believe it is quite defensible to do so; analogies add extra dimensions.
	There are instances where, at a dinner party of like-minded individuals, the sheer compatibility of guests, food and wines will spark off conversation of a high order. The possibility that a profusion of abstract similes, analogies, evocations, richly enlightening at the time, would, if recorded, sound pretty flat the next morning is immaterial.
	A fine example of evocative writing, neatly bridging the gap between the French and English approach to wine, was the late André Simon. In the opening issue of the *Quarterly Journal of the Wine and Food*

*Lehrer quoting, source not stated.

Society was recorded the first of many 'memorable meals'. It took place at the Hind's Head at Bray. At the end of the dinner the host, Barry Neame, asked André for his first reaction to the wines. He answered that his 'first thoughts evoked memories of Berkshire'. A 1926 Chablis – this was in 1934 – reminded him of 'the grace of the silver willow', the 1919 Montrachet 'of the stateliness of the Italian poplar', the 1920 Cheval-Blanc 'of the magnificence of the purple beech', the 1870 Lafite 'of the majesty of the Royal Oak'. But as to the brandy (an 1842 Roullet and Delamain) 'there was no tree with its roots in common clay to be mentioned in the same breath . . .'!

The wine snob

Out of a lesser man's mouth, with inapposite wines, without the touch of real poetry and, above all, without imaginative understanding, André's words would represent the quintessence of wine snobbery. Frankly, this is a term I try to avoid. But, alas, it is only too frequently used, equally by the ignorant and by the academic. As I believe the snob's main armoury is language, it is appropriate to raise the subject at this point.

If there *is* such a thing as a wine snob, he or she will have all the attributes of any other sort of snob: affectation and pretentiousness covering up the lack of everything that makes a person worthy of serious attention. The aristocrat of the table, the nature's gentleman of the cellar, the true *amateur*, the deeply knowledgeable, is rarely, if ever, a snob.

Those who are modest, undogmatic, listen to others' opinions and are honest in their own opinions, should be safe from the brickbats of the envious and ignorant. Those who are knowledgeable about wine should merely be careful on what occasion and in whose company they air their opinions and display their scholarship.

The wine bore

People who say little or nothing are not 'bores', just boring. It is the man of words (woman equally) who is at risk. A great expert can be a bore, particularly if speaking out of context, being repetitive, pedantic, opinionated, never listening to others or merely intoning in a tedious, grinding, long-winded way.

The wine bore is the person who talks about wine when no one is inclined to listen, or to the exclusion of all else. The answer is to try, not always easy, to open up one's hobby-horse or business only in the presence of those who are interested, and, if possible, to pre-judge the level of that interest.

Context of tasting

The trouble is, all those who talk about wine lay themselves wide open. If we talk of what we know not, to impress, we are wine snobs; if we talk of what we know, wine bores. Let us therefore forget these pejorative terms and concentrate on building up our knowledge, and on the correct use of words. 'Context' has cropped up many times in this chapter. It happens to be the crux of the problem. The *context* in which wine is tasted, and talked about, is of the greatest importance.

The occasion

(i) As stated earlier, tasting occasions, opportunities and settings, vary. The same wine may be viewed in a different light, and one's impressions and notes can differ.

Time and timing

(ii) Tiredness, a rushed tasting, will affect one's judgment and reduce the value of the tasting notes.

Service of wine	(iii) Wine served too warm or too cold, or tasted in too warm or too cold a room, will taste differently. Wines served in one order might taste slightly differently from the same wines in a different order (see Chapter III).
Lighting and colour	(iv) The effects of natural and artificial lighting were discussed in Chapter V. Professor Pusais* has conducted experiments leading him to conclude that certain wall colours will make a wine taste sweeter or more acid.
Personal influences	(v) A dominant personality, or a dogmatic one, can make one's judgment waver. One could go on. The point is that the senses, being delicate, are swayed by a multiplicity of outside factors. The impressions and the notes will reflect these, and one must be conscious of influences, if necessary, counter or allow for them. After all, we are only human!

Subjective or objective tasting

This brings me to a point which, I am sure, will be contentious. After a quarter of a century of tasting and teaching I am pretty well convinced that to talk about, let alone claim, total objectivity – 'relating entirely to the external object' – in tasting is nonsense. Moreover, to be a subjective taster is not a thing to be ashamed of. One could argue that a subjective approach – 'arising out of the senses' – is the most enriching approach to *fine* wine. The problem is, as usual, to note or convey both subjective and objective impressions, using words which can be understood. The sole *object* of one's concentration should be the wine, but in the final analysis 'I, the taster', am the final arbiter.

Judgment and taste thresholds

There are two areas in which judgment is required, at the commercial level and at the 'amateur' (in the French sense). At the commercial level, a merchant, with or without formal training, will taste and use his judgment; will note and convey information about the wine to his customers. At wine festivals and shows, where wine is tasted competitively, the judges must work out a common approach and system of assessing wines. The more equal in quality and style the wines are, the more precisely the basis of judgment must be defined. When it comes to detecting small differences, particularly in wines of neutral character, the sensory thresholds (the level at which elements of smell and taste can be detected) of the judges is important. It would be sensible to test these; and it is possible to do so (see Amerine and Roessler, p. 106).

Quantifying taste

I cannot subscribe to the dictum that, in effect, nothing is worth knowing unless it can be expressed numerically; indeed, in respect of *fine* wine I cannot help feeling that a pre-occupation with numbers merely serves to divert the taster from the true appreciation of facets of quality and style.

Having said this I can see little harm in allocating marks (see Chapter XI) to wines, so long as it is realised that a simple 'out-of-ten' (twenty or a hundred) score is only one taster's judgment of a given wine, in the context of a range of wines, in given company, on a particular day. It will merely serve to underline and summarise impressions and notes. Allocating a simple numerical rating also obliges one to come to a conclusion.

Directeur du Laboratoire Départemental et Régional d'Analyses et des Recherches, Tours.

| Averaging scores | Beware: to take the average of the scores or marks of a number of tasters, particularly if they are many and varied in experience and ability, can be highly misleading. It can reduce to a blurred middle-of-the-road sector both outstandingly-good and below-average, even faulty, wines. An over-generous scorer will neutralise a highly critical one. |

Statistical procedures

The French and American academics' partiality to algebra is altogether another thing. The object of the scientist and mathematician is to reduce the chance element in tasting. In effect, one eliminates as far as possible all the conditions which induce the varying subjective impressions I have already referred to, and, after testing the tasters, analyses the results statistically. I concede that with certain types of wine and in certain circumstances there is a case to be made, but it is generally beyond the level of knowledge and out of the area of interest of most wine lovers, in or out of the trade.

Summing up

Be honest with yourself. Try and express your impressions but be particularly careful in the use of words if you need to note particular factors, convey them to a third person or recognise them again yourself.

Frankly the subdivisions are infinite. One can argue endlessly about what words should be used. What sounds fatuous to one person may be totally acceptable to, and perfectly understood by, another.

There are no hard-and-fast rules. Words will vary from person to person, group to group; they will depend on usage, on teaching. Some will come into favour, some will fall out of favour.

In a social context, with good wines and like-minded people, loosen up: don't be afraid to express an opinion or a preference; let your imagination roam. Comments which are evocative help open up vistas for others, and aid the overall appreciation and mental 'digestion' of the wine. It is not so much precision that is required but a vital exchange of reactions and ideas, enabling so much more to be revealed, so much more to be gained.

In the final analysis, words should be used to illuminate and to enlighten; and they *must* be used as meaningfully as possible. If in doubt, refer to the following glossary. Check what *you* think you mean by what – let me be honest – *I* think I mean. You might not agree with all the definitions. At least they might give food for thought. Lastly, try to use words in the correct context, and qualify them when necessary.

Basic descriptive and 'danger' words

On the following two pages I have listed basic tasting words and impressions.

On the first page, basic descriptive words in the order of tasting any red and white wine; on the second, a list of words in common use, those which need qualifying, those to use with care and additional qualitative adjectives.

Refer to the glossary, Appendix i, for definitions.

Basic descriptive words in the order of tasting

RED WINES

Appearance

depth: very light (VL)★, light (L), medium-light (ML), medium-full (MF), full (F) or deep, very full (VF) or deep, opaque

colour/hue: purple, purple-rimmed, ruby, red, tile-red, brown-tinged, red-brown, mahogany

clarity: bright, lacking brightness, bitty, hazy, cloudy; light or heavy sediment

Nose or bouquet

condition: clean, unclean (sulphury, oxidized etc.)

fruit: fruity, lacking fruit, varietal, named variety

development: dumb, immature, undeveloped, well-developed, forthcoming, very mature

quality: poor, ordinary, good, fine, great, magnificent

Palate

apparent dryness: (noticeably) dry; slightly or unusually sweet (for a red wine); tannic

body: very light (VL)★, light (L), medium-light (ML), medium (M), full-bodied (F), heavy

tannin: mellow, noticably drying, marked

acid: supple, soft, refreshing, marked, over-acid, tart

fruit, flavour: fruity, lacking fruit; vinous; very flavoury, lacking flavour
   Describe flavour – use analogies when appropriate

development: well-developed, very mature, mature, beginning to mature, undeveloped, green

overall balance: well-balanced, unbalanced

length and finish: long flavour, short; lingering, fine aftertaste

WHITE WINES

Slight difference of emphasis, particularly regarding colour and sweetness:

Appearance

depth: colourless, very pale, medium, deep

colour/hue: green-tinged, yellow-green, yellow, straw, yellow-gold, gold, amber, deep gold, brown

clarity: starbright, bright . . . dull, cloudy

Nose or bouquet

more or less as for red wines

Palate

dry/sweet: bone dry, dry, medium-dry, medium-sweet, sweet, very sweet

body, acidity, fruit, development, balance, finish – more or less as for red wines. Tannin is not normally a factor in white wines.

★I use abbreviations in my own notes. The possible confusion between initials is avoided by tasting, and using words, in a regular order and under appropriate headings. Under 'palate', D, MF indicates 'dry, medium-full bodied'. Other abbreviations I use: fl. (flavour), bal. (balance), Y (young/youthful), V/A (volatile acidity), B/A (bottle-age), mat. (mature), ex (excellent), t & a (tannin & acidity), and so forth.

Words used in the description of wine, by category

Words in common

acid/acidity	finish	soft
aroma	fruity	sweet
balance/well-balanced	grapey	tannin, tannic
bouquet	hard	tough
clean	harsh	vinegary
dry/medium-dry etc.	poor	watery
	refreshing	

Words which need qualifying

aftertaste	flat	ordinary
big	full	penetrating
bland	heavy	peppery
body	light	positive
bright	little	refreshing
character	long	rich
coarse	mature/maturity	round
dull	meaty	sour
fat	medium-	strong
fine	neutral	weak
		youthful

Words to use with care

astringent	flinty	robust
baked	forthcoming	rough
bite	green	sharp
bitter	iron	smoky
corked	maderised	stalky
dumb	mouldy	tart
earthy	nutty	tang/tangy
extract	oxidized	varietal
feminine	piquant	vinous, vinosity
flabby	pungent	woody
		zesty/zestful

Additional qualitative descriptions

aromatic	mellow	silky
breed, well-bred	metallic	smooth
complex	musty	spicy
distinguished	noble	subtle
elegant	perfumed	supple
finesse	powerful	unripe
flowery	raw	velvety
fragrant	ripe	well-developed
insipid	scented	yeasty
luscious	sensuous	

Appendix i: Full glossary of tasting terms

acetic vinegary smell; sharp, over-tart on the palate. A vinegary condition resulting from the action of acetobacter, harmful ferments that attack wine left open in bottle, or fermented at too high a temperature, or carelessly bottled. Ullaged wine, whether in cask or bottle, will usually be suspect. The latter is usually due to poor, wormy or dried-out corks, which let air in and wine out (weepers), the remaining wine often becoming acetic and undrinkable.

acid, acidity on the nose: mouth-watering, refreshing (tartaric), sometimes like raw cooking apples (malic); detectable on the tongue, giving wine essential crispness and zing. 'Volatile' acids are more pronounced on the nose, 'fixed' acids (tartaric, succinic and citric) less so. Esters of both acids make an important contribution to the overall bouquet of wine. There are several types and degrees of acidity commonly found in wine, some beneficial and some detrimental. The right sort of natural acidity is an essential component part of a sound wine; it acts as a preservative, produces bouquet and provides the essential bite and finish. It also stimulates the gastric juices – one of the oft-forgotten main purposes of any table wine. Lack of acidity can be detected by a general flabbiness, lack of vitality and a weak watery finish; excess acidity by a sharp tart effect on the tongue. Youthful acidity tends to mellow with age. Some wines, such as *Vinho Verde*, Champagne, and wines from the Saar and Ruwer, have a deliberately and refreshingly-high acid content. Fruity acidity is perhaps the most desired characteristic of German wines. (See also TARTARIC, MALIC and SORBIC.)

aftertaste 'the internal bouquet' that sometimes remains in the throat and back nasal passages after a wine has been drunk. Unpleasant if the wine is strong-flavoured and in poor condition; at its best, however, the hallmark of a great wine and usually part of what is more poetically referred to as a 'lingering farewell'.

alcohol in *pure* form the higher alcohols, amyl and butyl, have unpleasant, throat-catching odour, phenethyl has an intense rose-like smell and ethanol a burning sensation. However, diluted, as in wine, alcohol is scarcely detectable on the nose,

though it can be assessed by its 'weight' in the mouth, by a sort of burning taste and, cumulatively, by its well-known effects on the head of the imbiber. Although table wines may vary only three degrees (3% by volume), from light Moselles around 11° to Rhône and Sauternes in the 13° to 14° bracket, the effect on the weight, character and strength of the wine is most marked.

almonds, bitter The smell of almond kernels or bitter almonds emanates from a badly fined wine, possibly 'blue' fined. Probably drinkable but not sound.

apples a fresh, raw smell, indicative of an immature young wine (see MALIC ACID).

aroma that part of the smell of wine derived from the grape, whether distinctly varietal or merely vinous (oenologists also use the word in respect of odours resulting from fermentation) as opposed to BOUQUET (q.v.) derived from development of the wine itself in bottle.

aromatic fragrant, implying a richness of aroma, possibly spicy overtones.

asbestos an odour imparted by badly kept, dirty or over-used filter pads in bottling. It leaves the wine flat, with an alkaline taste.

astringent a dry, mouth-puckering effect caused by a high tannin content (often accompanied by a high degree of acidity). Might well soften and mellow as the wine matures. Not bitter.

austere somewhat tough and severe; simple ie un-complex, possibly un-developed.

baked a 'hot' rather earthy smell produced by burnt and shrivelled grapes due to excessive sunshine and lack of rainfall. A characteristic of red wine produced in hot vintages in the Rhône Valley and in naturally-hot wine-producing areas such as southern California, Australia and South Africa.

balance the combination and relationship of component parts. (See WELL-BALANCED.)

banana overtone on the bouquet of wines made from frost-bitten grapes; also a specific smell of old wine in poor condition.

beery an undesirable smell caused by secondary fermentation in bottle. The wine may be drinkable, just, but will be basically unsound, poor on finish.

beetroot, boiled reminiscent of, and recognition symbol for, the *pinot* grape aroma.

big a wine full of flavour and high in alcohol, tannin, acidity and extract.

bite inferring a substantial degree of acidity (plus tannin). A good factor in a young wine. Generally mellows with age.

bitter, bitterness detected on the palate, on the back of the tongue and finish. Mainly unpleasant. A taste, not a tactile, sensation, though it can be a desirable quality in certain wines (usually an acquired taste) and vermouths. Bitterness is derived from either chemical salts or vegetable extracts. A certain bitterness can be imparted by colouring matter, though the depositing of this during maturation will normally reduce its pristine harshness. Polyphenols extracted from wooden casks, particularly when dirty and contaminated, will also, when oxidised, impart a bitter taste to wine. More rarely an unpleasant bitterness due to *amertume*, a bacteriological disease.

bitters substances added to wine (for example, in the making of vermouth) that have a bitter taste and stimulate the appetite and digestion. They can be of vegetable origin, like gentian, or aromatic, containing volatile oil, like orange peel. Quinine has a similar effect, plus additional properties such as a remote action on the nervous system.

blackcurrants the nearest fruit-smell to the *cabernet-sauvignon* grape. Detectable in some degree wherever the grape is used but particularly marked on wines from Pauillac, and to a slightly lesser extent Margaux. Perhaps the first major clue to Bordeaux wine in a blind tasting.

bland not complimentary: mild, easy, characterless; not unpleasing.

body the weight of wine in the mouth due to its alcoholic content, extract, and to its other physical components. These factors stem from the quality of the vintage and geographical origin, and in turn affect the style and quality of the wine. Wines from hotter climates tend to have more body than those from the north (compare the Rhône with the Moselle, for example).

bottle-age extremely hard to describe but easily recognizable on the bouquet to an experienced taster and a vital factor in the judgment of a wine's age/maturity and development in bottle. On white dessert wines a mellow, honeyed quality; on reds a breaking down of raw edges to reveal forthcoming softness and mellowness.

bottle-sickness temporary oxidation after bottling, which wears off.

bouquet in the broadest and often-used sense, the pleasant and characteristic smell of wine. In the narrower sense, the odour created by the wine's own development: by the esters and aldehydes formed by the slow oxidation of fruit acids and alcohol. (See also AROMA).

breed a distinctive and distinguished quality stemming from the combination of fine site, soil, *cépage* and the skill of the *vigneron*.

buttery self-descriptive smell and taste (not texture).

caramel a slightly burnt, toffee-like flavour which can have a literal origin in the case of certain spirits but can only be reminiscent in the case of wine. A characteristic flavour of madeira and marsala, for example.

carbon dioxide responsible for the sparkle of champagne and sparkling wines and the tingle of *spritzig* or slightly effervescent table wines.

cedarwood characteristic scent of many fine clarets.

character a wine of any quality which has unmistakable and distinctive features.

characteristic having the style and character of the grape, district, vintage, etc. Often sweepingly used to avoid a detailed description.

clean absence of foreign and unpleasant odours.

cloying a sweet and heavy wine which palls; lacking the acidity to make it crisp and interesting.

coarse rough texture; lacking breed and possibly indifferently made. Do not confuse coarseness with the rough rawness of a fine but completely immature wine.

common lacking breed, but none-the-less sound and drinkable.

complex many-faceted smell and taste. The hallmark of a developing fine wine.

cooked a heavy, sweet but not unpleasant smell indicating the use of sugar or concentrated must during vinification.

corked an 'off', oxidised and thoroughly obnoxious smell. A very over-used and misunderstood expression; the *sommelier's* nightmare.

corkey having a distinct smell of cork, arising from a poor, soft or distintegrating cork, or one infected by weevil. A poor cork can, of course, let air in, in which case the wine may oxidise completely and become 'corked'. Indeed, the two expressions are frequently interchanged due to lack of agreement over definition.

creaming a light, slightly frothy *mousse*. Half-sparkling.

crisp a desirable feature in white wines; firm, refreshing, positive acidity.

deep the sort of bouquet which reveals many layers of quality. The opposite to superficial.

delicate charm and balance in a light wine of some quality.

depth richness, subtlety – seemingly 'layers' of flavour, all interlocked.

developed in relation to wine is a maturity stage: un-developed, well-developed (mature, balanced, rounded), over-developed (over-mature, cracking-up).

distinguished marked and exceptional character and breed.

dry not sweet; absence of residual sugar; fully fermented out.

dull uninteresting. Probably insipid but sound.

dumb undeveloped, but with inherent promise of quality. Often the sign of an 'adolescent' stage.

dusty an evocative cellar-like smell; possibly high tannic content.

earthy characteristic overtone derived from certain soils.

eggs, bad (hydrogen sulphide) disagreeable, but harmless. Probably due to bad cellar-treatment.

elegant stylish balance and refined quality.

extract soluble solids (strictly speaking excluding sugar) which add to a wine's body and substance.

fat fullish body, high in glycerol and extract. If sweet, verging on unctuous.

feminine subjective and abstract term indicating a style of wine which is attractive, not heavy or severe, with charm—whatever delightful qualities all but a misogynist might conjure up!

filter-pads see ASBESTOS.

fine an all-embracing expression of superior quality. Perhaps the most overworked adjective in the vinous vocabulary.

finesse grace, delicacy, breed, distinction.

finish the end-taste. A wine cannot be considered well-balanced without a good finish, by which is understood a firm, crisp and distinctive end. The opposite, a short or poor finish, will be watery, the flavour not sustained and tailing off inconclusively. The correct degree of the right sort of acidity is a decisive factor.

firm implies a sound constitution and balance, positive in the mouth, as opposed to flabby.

flabby feeble, lacking crisp acidity, probably without finish. Either a poor wine or one that is cracking up.

flat dull, insipid, lacking acidity. Or merely a sparkling wine which has lost its sparkle.

flinty an evocative overtone. Certain white wine grapes grown on certain soils have a hint of gun-flint in the bouquet and flavour, e.g. Pouilly blanc fumé.

flowery fragrant, flower-like. Certain Moselles in 'full bloom', for example.

forceful marked character, probably well-endowed with tannin and acidity; assertive.

foxy the curious and distinctive earthy tang, flavour and finish of wine made from native American vine species. It does not imply an animal smell but relates to the wild or 'fox' grapes.

fragrant attractively and naturally scented.

fresh retaining natural youthful charm, vitality (and acidity).

fruity attractive, fleshy quality derived from good ripe grapes; but not necessarily a grapey aroma.

full (bodied) high in alcoholic content and extract. Filling the mouth. A table wine with an alcoholic content probably over 13° G.L. (i.e. per cent. alcohol by volume). In the context of fortified wines a heavy Sherry, Port or Madeira at the top end of the alcohol and sugar scale.

garlic, wild a faint reminiscent whiff denoting the presence of sorbic acid.

gentle mild, pleasant, unassertive.

geraniums not a complimentary flower simile: a geranium-like odour caused by the presence of an obscure micro-organism derived principally from esters formed during fermentation.

goaty a reference to a rich ripe animal-like flavour. For example, ripe fat Pfalz wines made from the *traminer* grape.

graceful abstract: elegant, unassertive, stylish.

grapey a rich *muscatelle*-like aroma produced by certain grape varieties, including *muscatelle* itself and crossings like *scheureube* and *müller-thurgau*.

great almost as over-worked as fine. Should be confined to wines of the highest quality which, in practice, means top growths of good years: having depth, richness, character, style, complexity, fragrance, length and aftertaste.

green unripe, raw and young. Youthful mouth-watering acidity produced by immature grapes, or the unsettled acidity of an immature wine.

grip a firm and emphatic combination of physical characteristics. A satisfactory and desirable quality in port, for example. The opposite to flabbiness and spinelessness.

hard severity due to the over-prominence of tannin and, to a lesser extent, acidity. Usually the product of a hot vintage or over-prolonged contact with skins and pips during fermentation. Time usually mellows.

harsh self-descriptive. Due to excess tannin and/or ethyl-acetate associated with acetic acid.

heady high in alcohol. Tipsy-making.

hearty robust, zestful, warm, alcoholic; generally in respect of red wine.

heavy more than just full-bodied; over-endowed with alcohol and extracts. Watch out for the context in which it is used. For example, a strapping Rhône wine will appear too heavy for a light summer luncheon but would be the right weight to accompany a steak and kidney pie in mid-winter. 'Heavy' is also an official definition: a fortified wine subject to the higher rates of duty.

hedonistic a simple subjective, personal rating e.g. pleasant to the individual taster.

hollow a wine with a fore-taste and some finish but without sustaining middle-flavour. A failing rather than a fault.

honest a somewhat condescending term for a decent, well-made but fairly ordinary wine.

honeyed characteristic fragrance of certain fine mature wines such as Sauternes and *Beerenauslesen*; indicative of bottle-age.

implicitly sweet   apparent sweetness from other sources than sugar, e.g. glycerol.

inky   'Red ink': an unpleasant, tinny, metallic taste due to the presence of tannate of iron produced by the action of tannin on iron – a nail in a cask will have this effect. Tannate of iron happens to be the chief constituent of ink.

insipid   flat, somewhat tasteless. Lacking firmness, character.

iron   a faintly metallic, earthy-iron taste derived from the soil. Noticeable in some St.-Emilions and in these circumstances natural, adding recognisable character.

legs   the English term for globules which fall down the sides of the glass after the wine is swirled. Also known as 'tears'. Generally indicative of a rich wine (see also page 24).

lemon   lemon-like overtones. For example, noticeable on some fine but immature white Hermitage wines.

light   a low degree of alcohol (under 12° G.L.). Lack of body. A desirable characteristic of certain styles of wine like young Beaujolais and Mosel-Saar-Ruwer wines. Rather confusingly, 'light' is an official term for a natural, unfortified, table wine.

limpid   clear (appearance).

limpidity   colour appears to have extra sheen, outstanding brightness.

little   scarcely any bouquet or aroma. Either a wine of no quality or character, or DUMB (q.v.).

lively   fairly explicit. Usually in reference to a fresh, youthful wine; or an old wine with fresh and youthful characteristics.

long   lingering flavour; a sign of quality.

luscious   soft, sweet, fat, fruity and ripe. All these qualities in balance.

maderised   the heavy flat smell of an over-mature, somewhat oxidised white wine (sometimes accompanied by brown-tinged colour and flat taste). See also OXIDISED.

malic acid   similar in character and effect to the smell of raw cooking apples: mouth-watering. Excess malic acid arises out of a preponderance of unripe grapes in the must which, if untreated, may lead to secondary fermentation in bottle. A 'malolactic' fermentation in cask converts the raw malic acid into softer and more amenable lactic acid.

manly   or masculine: positive, possibly assertive, even aggressive; a big wine, 'muscular'.

meaty   heavy, rich almost 'chewable' quality.

medium (body)   neither light nor heavy in alcohol and extract – probably between 12° and 13° G.L., depending on the style of wine.

medium-dry   containing some residual sugar but dry enough to be drunk before or during a meal.

medium-sweet   considerable natural sugar, but not really a dessert-wine. Many German wines come into this category and are better drunk without food.

mellow   soft, limpid, mature. No rough edges. A characteristic which is normally associated with maturity and age.

metallic   tinny – not a pleasant quality (see also INKY). Usually due to some metallic contamination during wine-making, storage in cask, or bottling. If distinctly unpleasant and associated with a deepening of colour (of white wine) and a tawny deposit, due to copper contamination.

mouldy   an undesirable flavour imparted by rotten grapes or stale, unclean, casks, etc.

mousey   smell and taste, flat yet acetic. Sign of bacteriological disease, *tourne*, usually affecting only wine in cask.

mushroomy   specific smell of some very old wines.

musky   a difficult term: spicy/dusty.

must   unfermented grape juice.

musty   due to poor casks or a cork fault. If the latter, allow the wine to stand after pouring and the smell may wear off after only a few minutes.

neutral   without positive flavour or marked physical characteristics. A common feature of very many blended wines, from quite respectable commercial burgundy to litre-bottled carafe wine.

noble   indicates stature and breed; a wine of towering elegance.

nuance   having components reminiscent of specific smells, e.g. of almonds, of struck flint.

nutty   a crisp rounded flavour associated with full-bodied dry white wines like Corton-Charlemagne, or good quality amontillados. Fine old tawny port has a distinct smell of cobnuts.

oak   an important factor, particular in relation to fine wines. Oak casks impart an 'oaky' taste and smell, desirable in moderation, undesirable if over-apparent.

off-taste   unclean, tainted or diseased wine; though not necessarily undrinkable.

old   can be a factual statement or imply a state of bouquet and taste adversely affected by over-maturity. Lacking freshness.

olfactory   to do with the sense of smell and its perception.

ordinary   in wine terms is mildly derogatory: a wine of no pretensions or with no merit.

organoleptic   the testing, by use of the senses, in an analytical context, of wine and food.

oxidised   flat stale off-taste due to exposure to air.

peach-like   self-descriptive. Characteristic of the bouquet of certain German wines, notably ripe Moselles from the Ruwer district.

peardrops   an undesirable overtone sometimes noticeable on poorly made white wines of lesser vintages. Wine probably unstable and in dubious condition, but may be quite drinkable.

penetrating   powerful, with almost a physical effect on the nostrils. Almost certainly high in alcohol and volatile esters.

peppery   a sort of raw harshness, rather hard to define, due to immature and unsettled component parts which have not had time to marry. Noticeable on young ruby and vintage port and many full young red wines. Probably higher alcohols.

perfume   an agreeable scented quality of bouquet.

piquant   fresh and mouthwatering acidity. A desirable and customary feature of wines from the Moselle, Saar and Ruwer and from other districts, like Sancerre. Less desirable but quite attractive in other youthful red and white table wines with a little more than their fair share of acidity.

poor   not 'off' or bad, but of no merit, character or quality.

positive   marked and noticeable, as opposed to LITTLE or DUMB q.v.

powerful   self explanatory, but more appropriately used in the context of a big red wine rather than a light white wine, a Rhine wine with a full, flowery bouquet.

pricked   an unpleasant sharpness due to excess volatile acidity. A pricked wine will not be pleasant to drink and will be beyond treatment. It may *just* be drinkable and will not have reached the final vinegary stage.

prickly   indicates on nose, but particularly on the palate, a sharp-edged, raw, possibly almost effervescent quality. Only tolerable in certain circumstances: raw, young *Vinho Verde* and such-like.

puckering, mouth-   a tactile sensation induced by high tannin content.

pungent   powerful, assertive, heavily-scented or spicy, very often indicating a high degree of volatile acidity as in old madeira.

quality   three senses: quality wine, like **fine** wine can be a vague and general term, often abused. In the E.E.C. 'quality' wines are legally defined, with statutory minimum criteria. In the abstract sense, a wine exhibits quality by virtue of its correctness, refinement and clarity of colour; its pure varietal aroma with harmonious overtones of bouquet; with all its component parts well-balanced, with rich and complex flavour, long finish and fragrant aftertaste.

refreshing   pleasant, thirst-quenching acidity.

resinous   literally imparted by the addition of resin, mainly to Greek table wines. A very old practice but something of an acquired taste.

rich   self-explanatory. Should not automatically imply sweetness, rather a full ensemble of fruit, flavour, alcohol and extract.

ripe   wine in full bloom, having reached its maturity plateau. A mellowness prior to its decline.

Ripe grapes give a wine a natural sweetness and richness.

robust   full-bodied, tough yet rounded. A good strapping mouthful of wine. Could apply equally to a 13.5° Châteauneuf-du-Pape or Taylor '48.

rough   a coarse, edgy sort of wine, usually of ordinary quality.

round   a feature of a well-balanced, usually mature, wine. No raw immature edges.

rubbery   probably presence of mercaptan, a disagreeable 'accident' of complex chemical background, not infrequently seen on old white wines due to the breakdown of sulphur.

rugged   big, masculine, high in alcohol, probably tannic.

salty   one of the so-called four primary tastes, but perhaps the least applicable to wine. A self-descriptive tang characteristic of good fresh manzanilla.

sap   the little-used equivalent of a somewhat enigmatic French term implying the quality of inherent life that will develop a fine young wine.

savoury   rich, spicy; mouth-smacking flavouriness.

scented   positive, grapey-flowery, high-toned aroma.

sensuous   rich, smooth, opulent flavour and texture.

severe   hard, unyielding and probably immature.

sharp   a degree of acidity between piquant and pricked. Implies a stage beyond that of being attractively refreshing. It could, however, become mollified with bottle-age.

sick   diseased, out of condition.

silky   a firm yet distinctly soft texture on the palate. A characteristic of most really fine dessert wines, also of good quality Pomerols.

simple   better than ordinary. Straight-forward, un-complex.

smoky   a subtle overtone characteristic of some grapes in certain white wine districts, e.g. good *pinot-chardonnay*. See also FLINTY.

smooth   soft, easy texture. No rough edges.

soft   self-descriptive. Mellow; no rough edges; tannin and acidity fully married and absorbed.

solid   full-bodied, four-square, packed with alcohol, tannin and acidity. Undeveloped.

sorbic acid   not a natural grape acid but one sometimes added as a preservative. Its presence can be detected by a faint garlic-like odour.

sound   the first thing a wine should be: appearance clear and bright; wholesome, clean bouquet and flavour. No faults.

sour   a term to be used with care. To the English, sour has an off-taste, over-acid connotation. Others use the word as a synonym for acid.

sparkling   a wine containing an induced degree of effervescence – the basis and whole point of a certain class of wine, such as champagne, the sparkle being obtained by the controlled release of carbon-dioxide when the bottle is opened.

spicy a rich, herb-like aroma and flavour bestowed by certain grape varieties such as *gewürztraminer*.

stalky reminiscent of the smell of damp twigs; a damp *chai*-like smell. This stalky or stemmy aroma is detectable in young wines and can arise from overprolonged contact with grape stalks during wine making.

stimulus that which provokes a sensory response.

strange untypical, having a 'foreign' smell or taste.

strong powerful, alcoholic.

sturdy fairly tough, substantial.

suave soft, supple and harmonious.

subtle veiled richness, unobvious complexity.

sugared/sugary several connotations: a sweet smell and blandness of a *chaptalised* wine; high sucrose content of a rich dessert wine.

sulphury sulphur, in its various forms, not only has a very pronounced volcanic smell but its presence can be detected physically by a prickly sensation in the nostrils and the back of the throat, like a whiff from a sulphur match or coke oven. It is commonly used as an antiseptic, for cleaning casks (by burning sulphur sticks) and bottles (using a mild SO_2 solution) and if carelessly used or over-used its undesirable odour will be retained. The bouquet of many young wines is masked by a whiff of sulphur which is quite harmless and often wears off a short while after the wine has been poured out.

superficial without depth or follow-through.

supple easy to taste and sense, hard to define. A combination of sap, vigour and amenable texture.

syrupy usually used in connection with an excessively rich, ripe Sauternes, *Trockenbeerenauslese* or perhaps sweet sherry.

sweet a wine with a high sugar content, natural or contrived. The essential characteristic of any dessert wine. There are two types of sweetness; that which is merely sweet and the other which is from the richness of fine, well-ripened grapes. The former kind will always remain sweet (e.g. Pedro Ximenez sherry), the latter will dry out as it ages. Fine Rhine wines and Sauternes can be recognized by the smell emanating from *pourriture noble* but even dry wines can have a 'sweet', honeyed or grapey sweetness on the nose. The principal sweetening elements are fructose, sucrose, glucose; also, but less sweet, glycerin and alcohol.

tactile that which provokes a response which can be physically felt (touched) e.g. sulphur, effervescence, velvety, creamy, burning (alcohol).

tang, tangy rich, high-toned, zestful bouquet and end-taste of an old madeira, old sherry, tokay.

tannin an essential preservative derived from grape skins during fermentation. Part of the maturation process consists of the breaking down of the tannin content; it is precipitated over a period by the action of proteins and becomes, with colouring matter, part of the deposit or crust left in the bottle. The presence of tannin dries the roof of the mouth, grips the teeth and sometimes has a 'dusty cellar' smell. It is a particularly noticeable physical component of young red wine (Bordeaux in particular) which has a practical purpose: to 'cut' fatty foods and clean the palate. Tannin is less of a factor in white wines as grape skins – the main source – are removed prior to fermentation.

tart sharp and tongue-curling due to over-acidity, often with a touch too much tannin. This condition can be due to premature harvesting of grapes or a late bad harvest. The wine could recover and soften; it may, on the other hand, disintegrate. More pronounced than PIQUANT (q.v.).

tartaric acid one of the good and essential acids in wine. Its chief virtue is the effervescent *spritzig* – cooling and refreshing – quality it provides (most marked in a good *Vinho Verde*, for example). Tartaric acid in the form of free acidity or acid tartrate of potassium is widely distributed in the vegetable kingdom but its chief source is the grape. Its presence gives wine its healthy, refreshing tang and contributes greatly to its quality and crisp finish. Occasionally it can be seen, as light white flakes, precipitated in white wine and sherry which have been subjected to an unusually low temperature.

taut somewhat severe, probably immature, firm, unyielding.

thin deficient in good natural properties; watery, lacking body.

threshold level at which a given smell or taste can be perceived. Thresholds vary from person to person, from substance to substance. It is possible with practice to lower (improve) olfactory and gustatory thresholds.

tough a full-bodied wine of overpowering immaturity (not necessarily young) with an excess of tannin. May well turn out in time to be a great wine.

twiggy like stalky and stemmy, a 'reminiscent' smell; mildly derogatory and usually relating to somewhat coarse young wines. A fine mature claret would never be described as twiggy. A raw young bourgeois one could.

un-balanced component parts ill-matched: over-tannic, over-acid, lacking fruit etc.

un-ripe two senses: immature, raw; 'green'; malic acidity of wine made from grapes not fully ripened.

vanilla purely descriptive in one sense, though it can be detected in a more literal sense in the bouquet of some brandies; a tannic-like compound derived from oak giving certain cask-aged wines a distinctive aroma.

velvety another textural connotation, related to silky and smooth, but implying more opulence.

vigorous lively, healthy, positive flavour associated with youthful development.

vinegar the smell of ethylacetate, one of the simple esters, indicative of bacteriological infection. The wine will be unfit to drink, acetic, and beyond redemption.

vinosity having firm, well-constituted, vinous character.

vinous a pleasant-enough and positive winey smell or taste.

volatile acidity this is present to a greater or lesser extent in all wine, but excess volatile acidity is undesirable and usually indicates the first step in acetic deterioration (see VINEGAR, above).

watery lacking fruit, extract, low in alcohol and acidity.

weak low in alcohol, feeble fruit and character.

well-balanced a satisfactory blend of physical components: fruit, acid, tannin, alcohol, etc., and, to a lesser extent, of the intangible elements: breed, character, finesse.

withered usually in reference to an old, dried-out wine, losing fruit and 'flesh' with age.

wood distinct and desirable odour derived from ageing in wooden casks (see also VANILLA).

woody an undesirable taste imparted by wine kept too long in cask.

yeasty descriptive smell of ferments, live or dead. If detected in bottled wine, a sure indication of impending or recent secondary fermentation.

young, youthful a positive attractive feature: fresh, with youthful acidity; immature.

Appendix ii: French tasting terms

acerbe acid; excessively sharp and bitter.
âcre harsh.
agressif raw, unripe, unharmonious.
aigre 'sour', vinegary, acetic acid taste.
aimable agreeable, nicely balanced.
amer, amertume bitter, disagreeable.
américain, goût fairly sweet (in relation to champagne). More vulgarly, implies a sugared-up blend of wine for the American market.
anglais, goût this depends on the district and context. In champagne, dry; in burgundy, big and smooth.
âpre rough, harsh; high tannin content.
arome aroma, relating to the perceived qualities arising from a particular grape variety, and so forth.
arrière-gout after-taste.
asescence a bacteria-caused disease causing over-acidity, leading to vinegar.
astringent astringent, tannic, mouth puckering.
bois, goût de woody taste, often the result of wine stored too long in a new cask.
bouchonné cork-tainted; smell of cork.
bouquet scent or perfume of a developing or mature wine.
bourru, vin new wine showing cloudiness prior to falling bright.
brut very dry (in relation to champagne, minimum liqueuring).
capiteux heady, high in alcohol.
casse showing cloudiness or darkening of colour usually due to metallic contamination.
charnu fleshy; full-bodied but with good acidity.
chaud 'warm', alcoholic.
chemise 'coating'- deposit on sides of bottle of old red wine.
chêne oaky character from the wood.
clairet light red, almost rosé.
classe wine of quality or potential.
complet balanced and harmonious.
corps body, robustness.
corsé full-bodied, well-constituted. Satisfactory but probably not mature in that state.
coulant pleasant, easy to drink.
coupé 'cut' i.e. blended or diluted.
court short, lacking balance.
crémant 'creaming'; slight sparkle.

creux hollow; momentary thinness on palate.
cuit, goût de wine with a 'cooked' flavour, or with a natural flavour resulting from a hot summer, or particularly hot soil.
cuit, vin 'cooked' flavour derived from addition of concentrated must.
dégustation tasting – the subject of this book.
délicat delicate; with a light consistency, usually on the low side in alcohol.
demi-sec 'half-dry' (in practice medium-sweet).
doux sweet.
dur hard; excess of tannin.
elégant elegant, stylish.
équilibré well-balanced, harmonious.
étoffé well-marked qualities and well conserved.
évent, goût d' nasty, unclean smell and flat taste.
éventé wine which has been abruptly over-oxidised, in bottle or cask.
faible weak, thin.
ferme firm; implying the dumb unreadiness of an immature fine wine.
ferment, goût de taste of a wine still fermenting; or in bottle having recently undergone a secondary fermentation; yeasty.
fin fine.
finesse grace, delicacy, breed, distinction.
fort strong.
frais fresh. In another context, cool.
franc natural, clean, sound.
français, goût sweet, particularly in relation to champagne.
fruité fruity.
fumet marked bouquet.
fusil, pierre à bouquet and/or taste reminiscent of gun flint.
garde, vin de good enough to lay-down, or which *should* be laid-down to mature.
généreux forthcoming; rich in body and extract.
goudron, goût de tarry taste.
goût taste. A term always qualified.
grain character; completeness.
graisse a diseased wine which is flat, faded and oily.
grossier big and coarse.
léger light in body and style.
liquoreux sweet and rich, implying a natural state.
long lingering flavour, intense and aromatic.

lourd heavy, dull, unbalanced.

mâche mashed: a disturbed, tired or unsettled wine.

maderisé maderised.

maigre meagre, thin and feeble.

mauvais goût bad taste; unfit to drink.

moelleux soft and rich, yet not necessarily sweet.

moisi, goût de musty taste.

mou flabby, flat, lacking in character.

mouillé watered.

mousse froth, foam, sparkle.

mousseux sparkling (fully, like champagne).

mout unfermented grape juice.

mûr balanced, in a mature state not in a youthful context.

muté muted; a must whose fermentation has been artificially arrested (leaving an unusually high unfermented sugar content).

nature, vin natural, unsugared wine.

nerveux firm, vigorous, vital; fine and well-knit.

odeur smell, in the simple direct sense: smell of cork, smell of wine, of yeast.

oeil de perdrix 'partridge eye'; descriptive of the tawny gold of certain types of wine.

onctueux full-bodied, fat and rich. Usually applies to sweet wines but not necessarily to the exclusion of red.

paille, goût de reminiscent of damp straw – not complimentary.

parfum perfume; fragrance. Term for grape aroma.

passé too old; going downhill (but may be drinkable, just).

pâteux thick pasty consistency.

pauvre poor, small.

pelure d'oignon the colour of onion skin. May apply to certain *vin gris* and some *rosé* wines; occasionally to old and maderised white wines.

perlant slight sparkle more akin to a prickle (similar to the German term *spritzig*).

pétillant light natural sparkle.

petit a little wine, probably deficient in alcohol and no great shakes.

piquant sharp and acid; may be an attractive tartness or purely derogatory, depending on context.

piqué pricked. Dangerous degree of volatile acidity in a wine on its death-bed.

piqûre a disease which creates a grey film on the surface of the wine, decomposing the alcohol into vinegar.

plat flat and dull.

plein full. Not just body but character.

précoce precocious. Early maturing.

race breed.

rancio, goût de smell characteristic of old *vin doux*. Usually involves a degree of oxidation and is something of an acquired taste.

riche generous.

robe colour; generally used in relation to that of a fine wine.

rond, rondeur round, harmonious.

rude astringent.

sauvage, goût taste imparted by native American vines and some hybrids.

saveur taste, in the mouth, in its broadest sense.

sec dry, fermented out.

séché dried-out; harsh and flat. Withered after lying ullaged in bottle or too long in cask.

sève sap: a combination of vigour, firmness, youthful charm and inherent quality.

solide substantial, full-bodied but well-balanced.

souple supple: no sharp edges; elegant balance, soft and pleasant to drink.

soyeux silky texture; supple, slightly plump.

spiritueux high in alcohol.

suave soft, supple, harmonious.

sucré a sweetness generally associated with arrested fermentation or some other less natural (i.e. added) degree of sugar.

taille, goût de raw, poor quality (after name for last pressing – the tail end).

tendre youthful delicacy. Charming: easy to drink; light and supple.

terne dull; lacking quality and interest.

terroir, goût de earthy smell and flavour derived from certain soils.

tourne a bacteriological disease that gives wine a dull appearance, a 'mousey' smell and makes it flat though acetic at the same time.

troublé 'troubled' (appearance): hazy, cloudy. Wine diseased, or temporarily out of condition.

tuilé of tile-red colour. A curious stage that a wine might reach having lost its youthful purple hue, showing a maturity which may not be long-lived.

usé worn-out; past best and on decline.

velouté velvety texture.

vert 'green' – unripe.

vif fresh, young and lively.

vineux having vinosity; also high in alcohol.

vivace fresh and lively, implying youthful zing and possibly a certain tartness.

Appendix iii: German tasting terms

angereichert sugared.

ansprechend appealing; attractive.

art character.

artig smooth, rounded.

beerenton taste of (ripe) grapes.

bitter bitter.

bleichert rosé. Rare in Germany and mainly found in the Ahr Valley, and Schillerwein.

blume bouquet.

blumig flowery; good.

bukettreich rich bouquet.

charaktervoll characterful.

delikat delicate.

duft fragrance.

edel noble, fine.

ehrwein very fine.

elegant elegant, stylish.

erdig earthy

fade insipid.

faul mouldy.

fein, feine fine.

feinste finest.

fett fat.

firn maderised.

fluchtig little to it.

frisch fresh.

fruchtig fruity.

fülle full, rich.

gefällig pleasing and harmonious.

gering poorish.

gewürz spice: spiciness – of bouquet or flavour.

gezuckert sugared.

glatt smooth.

grosse great, big.

grün green; unripe.

gut good.

hart hard and tart.

hebegeshmack yeasty taste.

herb bitter.

hochfeine very fine.

holzgeschmack woody taste.

honigartig honeyed.

hübsch handsome, pretty; nice, at least.

jung young.

kernig firm.

körper body.

körperarm lacking body.

kraftig robust.

lebendig racy.

leer weak in character.

lieblich pleasant.

mager thin; lacking body.

mandelbitter bitter-almond flavour.

matt flat.

milde pleasantly soft, middle of the road.

naturrein, naturwein pure, unsugared.

nervig full-bodied.

oelig of marked viscosity.

perle light natural sparkle.

pikant intriguing in tangy, spicy sense.

rafle stemmy: harsh and green.

rassig showing race; breeding.

rauh raw.

reif ripe.

rein pure.

reintönig harmonious; well-balanced.

rot red.

rund round, harmonious.

saftig 'juicy'.

sauber pure; clean.

schal musty.

schaumwein sparkling wine

schön lovely.

schwefel sulphur.

sekt sparkling wine.

spiel flexible, balanced.

spritzig with crisp natural prickle.

stahlig steely.

süffig not unlike *tendre* (fr.).

süss sweet.

trocken dry (in 'withered grape' sense).

ungezuckert unsugared; pure.

voll full.

vornehm exquisite, elegant, distinctive.

weinig high in alcohol.

wernig displaying vinosity.

wuchtig potent.

würzig spicy.

zukunft for the future. A wine capable of development and needing age.

Appendix iv: Italian tasting terms

abboccato with some sweetness.

acerbo taste of unripe apples.

aggressivo aggressive: raw, unripe, unharmonious.

allappante unpleasant, rough, ill-tempered.

amabile gentle, slightly sweet.

ammaccato with disagreeable taste, between dry and musty.

ammandorlato blend of semi-sweet and almond-bitter tastes.

ampio ample: complete and generous.

aristocratico aristocratic; wine of fine pedigree: good soil, vines, vinification and vintage year.

armonico harmoniously blended and enhanced flavours.

asciutto dry: fermented out, clean.

aspro rough on the palate.

astringente astringent.

austero austere: a characteristic of big young wines.

carattere a wine with distinction and typical character.

caratteristico with characteristic individual traits.

carezzevole caressing: rich, flowing.

completo complete.

con retrogusto with aftertaste.

corpo body: rich in alcohol and extracts.

costituito well-constituted.

debole a wine with little character.

deciso with decisive qualities.

decrepito old and faded.

delicato fine and harmonious.

di corpo full-bodied; with high alcoholic degree.

duro hard, excess tannin.

elegante elegant, stylish.

equilibrato well-balanced, harmonious.

erbaceo green, unripe, slightly piquant.

fiacco tired; lacking vigour.

franco blunt and straightforward. No subtleties.

fresco fresh in style, refreshing.

fruttato fruity.

generoso forthcoming; rich in body and extract.

grasso unctuous.

immaturo immature.

maderizzato, o marsalato maderised.

magro lean; lacking body.

marca of marked character (of grape, type, district).

morbido tender, gentle, soft and caressing in the mouth.

nerbo lit. nerve. A wine of fibre and inner strength.

nervoso sensitive, delicate yet vivacious.

netto clean cut; basic taste particularly marked.

neutro neutral: of little character, nearly always lacking sufficient acidity.

oleoso oily. Probably spoiled.

passabile acceptable, inoffensive.

pieno full: with richness and body.

pronta beva a quickly maturing young wine which should be drunk soon.

rotondo round: full and mellow.

ruvido rough, raw-tasting.

salato salty character.

sapido similar to the French term *sève*.

secco dry. Fermented out.

selvatico coarse uncivilised character.

spogliato spoiled, through over ageing.

stoffa applicable to great wines with mouth-filling many-faceted qualities.

tannico tannic.

vellutado velvety texture.

verde green, unripe.

vinoso vinous.

vuoto empty: superficial, short flavoured, no follow-through.

Appendix v: Books about wine

Wine writing

Books should add to one's knowledge *and* understanding of wine. There is a place for the discursive as well as the strictly factual book though the former is only tolerable if written with scholarship and style, and the latter only if accurate and unbiased.

The older breed of writers seemed to me more literary, more broadly civilised; the more recent tend to be more mundane purveyors of general information (and all too frequently second-hand opinions).

There is no denying that there has been a veritable spate of books on wine over the past ten years, some outstanding, few original, and many repetitive – for what new fact can a writer expose or what opinion can be expressed that is not already in print?

There would seem scarcely enough fresh material to fill a new book; yet books continue to appear, willing authors being encouraged by publishers anxious to feed a seemingly inexhaustibly-ravenous market. Not even the duplication of title seems to worry the bookseller, two 'Entertaining with Wine' appearing – in the U.K. and U.S.A. – within weeks of each other; two 'Wines of the World' within months.

Of latter-day authors, Hugh Johnson towers above the rest in his singular ability to master and assimilate facts and present them in a concise form, neatly wrapped and highly informative. Cyril Ray is one of the few remaining stylists: he understands and enjoys words. He composes and polishes. Now I come to think of it, he is also one of the few witty writers on wine. Being a simpleton myself, I find that academic writers write for fellow intellectuals and seem to be either incapable of making themselves clear to the layman or fearful of doing so lest their status is diminished.

Selection

I am not a book collector though, quite naturally, I have amassed quite a few volumes over the past twenty-five years. I used to read, from cover to cover, every book and every wine article I could lay my hands on, force-feeding myself as it were. Even though many were repetitive I was, and still am, grateful for a new insight or new perspective. I am less avid now, mainly because there are not enough hours in the day.

So the following list represents a very personal selection. It opens up with all the books that I have come across dealing directly with the subject of tasting, whether or not I agree with the techniques or opinions expressed; next come books that add to one's knowledge of wine, and those which fill out one's understanding – but the margin sub-titles speak for themselves. I have also included one or two libraries, specialised wine booksellers and, for the first time, wine magazines and major trade journals.

Layout

The title of the book and author(s) come first. The publisher and date of original publication appear in brackets, the second date being that of the latest edition, if applicable. The availability of a cheap or paper-back edition is indicated with a †. Finally, I have added a brief critique: after all, anyone who has the temerity to commit himself in writing is laying himself open to criticism, even if, like tasting, it tends to be subjective. But that is life! I am equally vulnerable.

Scientific approach to tasting

Modern Sensory Methods of Evaluating Wines by M. A. Amerine, E. B. Roessler and F. Filipello (Hilgardia, University of California, June 1959) – a scholarly pamphlet dealing with the senses, chemical components, statistical tasting techniques and mathematical scoring systems. One of the first modern treatises on the organoleptic examination of wine. Not for the amateur, even if he managed to obtain a copy.

Sensory Evaluation of Wines by M. A. Amerine and E. B. Roessler (Wine Institute, San Francisco, 1964) – a follow-up of *Modern Sensory Methods* but still concerned with the academic approach to product testing.

Wines, Their Sensory Evaluation by Maynard A. Amerine and Edward B. Roessler (Freeman and Company, San Francisco, 1976). Putting 'Wines' first, introducing the christian names of the authors and including an odd *New Yorker* cartoon or two is a clear indication of intent: a last-ditch effort of distinguished professors to meet lay-readers half-way. However, whereas at least half the book is still too complex for non-academics, the remainder is a must. Though some curious prejudices are exhibited, it is scholarly, informative and impressive.

On the senses

Odour Description and Odour Classification by R. Harper, E. C. Bate-Smith and D. G. Land (J. & A. Churchill, London, 1968) – very scientific review of systems and classifications.

The Human Senses in Action by Roland Harper (Churchill Livingstone, Edinburgh and London, 1972) – the structure of sense organs, nature of stimuli, methods of measuring perception; with an exhaustive bibliography. Dr. Harper, of Reading University, writes for fellow scientists; but *really* keen wine students might well find the book fascinating, as I did.

For keen buffs

How to Test and Improve Your Wine Judging Ability by Irving H. Marcus (Wine Publications, Berkeley, California, 1972†) – a small paper-back by the former owner-editor of *Wines and Vines*. The first part compact and helpful, the second a potted version of the Amerine-Roessler evaluation tests.

The Flavour of Wine by Dr. Max Lake (Jacaranda Press Pty. Ltd., Sydney, 1969†) – an attractive, original and sometimes complex little book by an erudite Australian surgeon-cum-winery owner.

In French

Essai sur la Dégustation des Vins by A. Vedel, G. Charle, P. Charnay and Journeau (S.E.I.V., Mâcon, 1972†) – a detailed and, for the lay reader, complicated tabulated treatise full of Gallic logic and thoroughness. Doubtless this impressive team was jolted into action by the appearance of an English author on *their* subject in a French wine journal!

Précis d'Initiation à la Dégustation by Jacques Puisais and R. L. Chabanon (Institute Technique du Vin, 1969†) – a detailed work by two distinguished French wine technicians.

Une Initiation à la Dégustation des Grands Vins by Max Léglise (Defense et Illustration des Vins d'Origine, Lausanne, 1976†) – a scholarly and richly interesting book by the Directeur de la Station Oenologique de Bourgogne à Beaune. Probably the best book in French on tasting.

Translated for Americans

Initiation into the Art of Wine Tasting by J. A. Vaccaro (Interpublish Inc., Madison, Wisconsin, 1974†). A rather laboured version of the *Précis* . . . by Puisais and Chabanon, well illustrated and interesting, but including the original irrelevant apple and cream-cracker score sheets and information about French hotel school courses.

Books with tasting a major feature

The Physiology of Taste by Brillat-Savarin (Peter Davies, London, 1925†) – a famous classic: discursive, civilised. Translated from the French *Physiologie du Goût*, 1825.

Notes on a Cellar Book by George Saintsbury (Macmillan, London, 1920) – detailed reminiscent jottings, which had a seminal influence on wine writing and connoisseurship.

A Matter of Taste, Wine and Wine Tasting by Jack Durac (André Deutsch, London, 1975) – a New York book reviewer incorrectly credited Mr. Durac, a research scientist at London University, with being 'the first' to make 'a systematic attempt at explaining how a wine should be tasted . . . ' etc. Appalling maps, stodgy production, some curious approaches, but full of information and earnest guidance.

The Taste of Wine by Pamela Vandyke-Price (Macdonald and Jane's, London, 1975) – sixty pages of highly original, not to say idiosyncratic, taste classifications flanked by less original general matter: wine making, maps and so forth. This book outlines the tasting approach of one professional writer. But there are other methods if this approach is not for you. Nevertheless, this one book contains a great deal of information, is attractively produced and very good value. If you wanted just *one* book on wine, this might fill the bill.

Harry Waugh's Wine Diaries (Christie's Wine Publications) – a series of travel journals and notes on tastings that started with *Bacchus on the Wing*, *The Changing Face of Wine* and *The Pick of the Bunch* (all by Wine and Spirit Publications, London, 1966, 1968 & 1970); *Diary of a Wine Taster* and *Winetaster's Choice* (both Quadrangle, New York, 1972 & 1973) and *Harry Waugh's Wine Diary Volume Six* and *Volume Seven* (Christie's Wine Publications, 1975 & 1976†) – personal, full of warmth, charm, enthusiasm and honestly expressed opinions on wines and vintages.

Gorman on California Premium Wines by Robert Gorman (Ten Speed Press, Berkeley, California, 1975†) – thoughtful and effective approach to tasting, with model notes.

Essential works of reference

The World Atlas of Wine by Hugh Johnson (Mitchell Beazley, 1971/1977) – comprehensive, exhaustive; invaluable to have at one's side whilst reading about or visiting wine districts. An astonishing wealth of information, inimitably presented. This is the book I would take to a desert island.

Encyclopaedia of Wines and Spirits by Alexis Lichine (Cassell, 1967/1977) – the other book to have at one's side. It is the encyclopaedia I like best and use most.

Encyclopaedia of Wine by Frank Schoonmaker (Hastings House, New York, 1964/1977).

Wine primers and all-rounders

A Wine Primer by André L. Simon (Michael Joseph, 1946/1972†). One of the first general books for the beginner, by the Master.

The Signet Book of Wine by Alexis Bespaloff (New American Library, 1971†) – deservedly a best-seller in the U.S.A. Nice direct style of writing and accurate information.

Wine by Hugh Johnson (Nelson, 1966/Mitchell Beazley, 1974†) – His first major book, in which he demonstrated his art of succinct 'distillation' and lucid presentation.

Wines and Spirits by L. W. Marrison (Pelican, 1957/Penguin, 1976†) – for many years my everyday general book on wine.

Teach yourself Wine by Robin Don M. W. (The English Universities Press, 1968/1977) – concise, informative.

Books on the wines of countries

The Wines of France by Alexis Lichine (Cassell, 1952/reprinting). Lichine's first, and always a favourite of mine. I like writers who express opinions, even if one does not always agree.

A Book of French Wines by Morton Shand (1928) revised by Cyril Ray (Penguin, 1964†).

German Wines by S. F. Hallgarten (Faber & Faber, 1976).

German Wines by Frank Schoonmaker (Oldbourne, London, 1957). I like the style and layout and still refer to it.

The Wines of Italy by Cyril Ray (McGraw-Hill, 1966).

Catalogo dei Vini d'Italia by Luigi Veronelli (Bolaffi, Milan, 1972). So well illustrated and presented that it is useful for non-Italians to refer to. Dr. Veronelli is Italy's leading wine-writer.

The Wines of Central and South-Eastern Europe by R. H. E. Gunyon (Duckworth, London, 1971) – about the only book on this area, by a now-retired English wine shipper.

The Wines of America by Leon D. Adams (Houghton Miffling, 1973). Comprehensive, erudite, readable, by the dean of American wine writers.

Australian and New Zealand Complete Book of Wines by Len Evans (Hamlyn, 1973/1976) – a fully comprehensive compilation by the outstanding wine personality of Australia.

The Classic Wines of Australia by Max Lake (Jacaranda Press, Australia, 1966/7).

About particular wine areas

The Wines of Bordeaux by Edmund Penning-Rowsell (Michael Joseph, revised 1976†) – definitive and exhaustive, by England's soundest and most respected commentator on claret and the wine market in general.

Bordeaux et Ses Vins (known, after the publishers, as 'Cocks et Feret', Bordeaux, 1969) – the 'bible' of Bordeaux, listing all the châteaux, great and small, by district. Vast index of properties and owners.

The Great Châteaux of Bordeaux by Hubrecht Duijker (Times Books, 1975) – original, comprehensive notes by Holland's leading young wine writer. Beautifully illustrated

Les Vins de Bourgogne by P. Poupon and P. Forgeot (Beaune, 1969†) – a small, authoritative, classic.

The Wines of Burgundy by H. W. Yoxall (Michael Joseph, 1968†) – wise and civilised, by a past-chairman of the Wine and Food Society.

Burgundy, Vines and Wines by John Arlott and Christopher Fielden (David Poynter, London, 1976) – two Englishmen, one, a leading journalist, the other a former sales director of a major burgundy house in Beaune, combine to produce a lively, informative treatise.

Alsace and Its Wine Gardens by S. F. Hallgarten (Wine and Spirit Publications, 1969).

Champagne by Patrick Forbes (Gollancz, 1967/1977) – definitive.

Sherry by Julian Jeffs (Faber and Faber, 1961/1970).

The Story of Port by Sarah Bradford (Christie's Wine Publications, 1978) – a new and revised edition of *The Englishman's Wine* (1969).

Madeira by Rubert Croft-Cooke (Putnam, 1961).

Monographs

Mouton-Rothschild by Cyril Ray (Christie's Wine Publications, 1974/7†) – by the master of the pen portrait, the 'elder-tasteman' of English wine writing.

Lafite by Cyril Ray (Peter Davies, 1971; new and revised edition, Christie's Wine Publications, 1978†).

Bollinger by Cyril Ray (Peter Davies, 1971).

Krug by John Arlott (Davis Poynter, 1976).

Historical and classical

Wines of the Ancients by Sir Edward Barry (London, 1775).

A History of Ancient and Modern Wines by Alexander Henderson (London, 1825).

A History and Description of Modern Wines by Cyrus Redding (London, 1833).

Wines, the Vine and the Cellar by T. G. Shaw (Longmans Green, 1863/4) – frankly my favourite. The wine travels of an energetic character with a lively and enquiring mind. We still have the same problems he encountered! Nothing changes.

Vintagewise by André L. Simon (Michael Joseph, 1945) – a civilised, erudite follow-up to Saintsbury's *Cellar Book*.

Dionysus, A Social History of Wine by Edward Hyams (Thames and Hudson, 1965) – a monumental work.

A History of Wine by H. Warner Allen (Faber and Faber 1961) – learned and literary: a style of writing no longer encountered.

Gods, Men and Wine by William Younger (Michael Joseph, 1966) – so is this. For those with time on their hands.

Jefferson and Wine (The Vinifera Wine Growers Association, The Plains, Virginia, U.S.A., 1976) – a fascinating study of America's wise, much-travelled first gentleman of wine.

Discursive semi-classics

Viniana by C. W. Berry (Constable, 1929) – and *In Search of Wine* by Charles Walter Berry (Constable, 1935) – not a travel book, the travels and jottings of a London wine merchant of the old-school.

Stay Me with Flagons by Maurice Healy (Michael Joseph, 1940) – lusty, articulate, anecdotal. No one writes like this now, more's the pity.

Wayward Tendrils of the Vine by Ian Maxwell Campbell (Chapman and Hall, 1948) – the reminiscences of a most eminent wine shipper.

Wine's My Line by T. A. Layton (Duckworth, 1955) – typical of the many books written by the brilliant and unpredictable Tommy.

Wine Libraries

The Guildhall Library, in the City of London, houses the Library of the Institute of Masters of Wine, which in turn incorporates the old Wine Trade Club Library, founded and amassed by André Simon. (Reference library open to the public.)

The Jack Harvey Memorial Library, forming part of the Harvey Wine Museum in Bristol, (well worth a *détour*, but by appointment only).

The Fresno State College Wine Library, California, incorporating the extensive library collected by Roy Brady, a former editor of *Wine World*.

The A. J. Winkler Library in the department of Viticulture and Enology, University of California, Davis.

Public Libraries: most public libraries in the United Kingdom have a food and wine section, and titles not stocked can usually be obtained, on request, through the scheme of inter-library loans which exists between libraries.

Specialist wine-book sellers

The Wine Book Club (Woodlands, Hazel Grove, Hindhead, Surrey, GU26 6BJ). Comprehensive lists, titles old and new.

Elizabeth Woodburn (Booknoll Farm, Hopewell, New Jersey, 08525, U.S.A.) – regular lists, food and wine.

The Wine and Food Library (Jan Longone, 1207 West Madison, Ann Arbor, Michigan 48103, U.S.A.).

Janet Clarke, Antiquarian Books (3 Woodside Cottages, Freshford, Bath, BA3 6EJ).

Wine magazines

Decanter (16 Black Friars Lane, London, EC4) – the best English monthly. The natural successor to the original *Wine* Magazine.

Wine World (15101 Keswick Street, Van Nuys, Ca. 91405, U.S.A.) – six issues per annum. Excellent content and production.

Vintage Magazine (245 East 25th Street, New York, N.Y. 10010, U.S.A.) – bi-monthly.

Wine (2302 Perkins Place, Silver Spring, Maryland 10910, U.S.A.) – the Journal of the *Les Amis du Vin* organisation of America.

The Journal of the International Wine and Food Society (104 Pall Mall, London, SW1) – a quarterly. One of the tangible rewards of membership of this old-established and prestigious society.

La Revue du Vin de France (6 Avenue du Coq, Paris 75009, France) – five issues per annum. Old-established, high-grade, with both French and English editions.

Vini (Via Sudorno 44, 24100 Bergamo Alta, Italy) – a glossy and lively wine and food monthly.

Wine trade journals

There are literally dozens of trade journals, varying from tabloid dailies (*The Morning Advertiser*) and weeklies (such as the *Off-Licence News*) to esoteric quarterlies. Most are of limited or local interest; many are vehicles for trade brand advertising, fine wines rarely being featured. Those of high quality and/or broader appeal are listed below:

Wine and Spirit (34 Foubert's Place, London, W1) – the leading British trade monthly. Vintage notes, world market notes and reports, summarised auction prices etc.

Harper's Wine and Spirit Trade Gazette (Harling House, 47-51 Great Suffolk Street, London, SE1) – old-established weekly, with up-to-date trade and market news, recent wine auction prices etc.

La Journée Vinicole (7 Rue Dom-Vaissette, 34 – Montpellier, France) – French monthly, with English-language 'export' issues.

Wines and Vines (703 Market Street, San Francisco, California 94103, U.S.A.) – monthly: trade news; emphasis on California wine production and market.

Wynboer (P.O. Box 528, Suider-Paarl, 7624 South Africa) – bi-lingual, English and Afrikaans, glossy monthly.

Christie's Wine Review (Christie's Wine Publications, 8 King Street, London, SW1) – annual review of wine market and fine wine prices; also articles for the connoisseur and collector.

Appendix vi: Acknowledgements

The following lists the many people, friends and firms, who have over the years provided me with tasting opportunities. In some instances just a single memorable meal at which I noted outstanding wines; in others, on several occasions and at wine society and company tastings.

Names have been gleaned from my – to date – thirty-five small tasting books over a period of exactly twenty-five years. Some old friends are no longer with us; some might well be surprised to see themselves included, and will rack their brains to remember the occasion. Others, undoubtedly may take offence at being omitted, for which an incomplete tasting record and my all-too-fallible memory must take the blame.

Anyway, to those who appear listed in the columns below, and to many others I have inadvertently left out, I am greatly indebted.

Abell, Tom
Adamson, Dr. Robert (*U.S.A.*)
Aldridge, Roger
Allan, David
Allen, Basil
Alment, Tony
d'Ambrumenil, David
Amerine, Dr. Maynard (*U.S.A.*)
d'Angludet, Château
Antinori, Marchese Piero (*Italy*)
Armit, John
Aschaffenburg, Lyle (*U.S.A.*)
Avery, John
Avery, the late Ronald

Bamford, Ian
Bamford, Martin
Barton, Ronald (*Bordeaux*)
Basmadjieff, L. A., (*Switzerland*)
Behrens, Michael
Berkmann, Joseph
Berry, Anthony
Bignall, Ken (*Australia*)
de Billy, Christian (*Champagne*)
Binaud, Henri (*Bordeaux*)
Bischoflisches Konvikt/Priesterseminar
Bise, Mme Leroy- (*Burgundy*)
Bizot, Christian (*Champagne*)
Blass, Wolf (*S. Australia*)
Blayney, Robert
Bouchard Père et Fils
Borie, Jean-Eugène (*Bordeaux*)
Bostock, Ian

Bourke, Mrs. K.C.
Brand, Eric (*Coonawarra, Australia*)
Bridgeman, Dick
Brown, John (*Milawa, Australia*)
Budin, Michel (*Champagne*)
von Bühl (*Rhine*)

Carpenter, Julia
Castéja, Emile (*Bordeaux*)
Chambers, Bill (*Rutherglen, Australia*)
Chance, I. O. (Peter)
Chapoutier, Max (*Rhône*)
Clark, Matthew & Sons
Clevely, John, M.W.
Cobb, Reggie (*Oporto*)
Cockburn's (*Oporto & London*)
Cordier (*Bordeaux*)
Cordier, Jean (*Bordeaux*)
Cordier, Madame (*Bordeaux*)
Cottin, Philippe (*Bordeaux*)
Crawshaw, Lord
Cruse, Edouard (*Bordeaux*)

Dancz, Pal (*Eger, Hungary*)
Davy, John
Deinhard & Co.
Delaforce, the late G.R. 'Wog'
Dickens, Dr. Will (*U.S.A.*)
Dolamore's
Dömötör, Joseph (*Budapest, Hungary*)
Don, Robin, M.W.
Doudet, Marcel (*Burgundy*)
Doudet-Naudin

Danglade, Patrick (*Bordeaux*)
Danglade, Roger (*Bordeaux*)
Dowglass, George, M.W.
Dreyfus, Ashby
Drouhin, Robert (*Burgundy*)
Druitt, Michael
Ducru-Beaucaillou, Château
Dugdale, David
Dyer, Maj-Gen. Max

Edmonds, Richard (*Boodle's*)
Elliott, the late Brian
Eltz, Schloss
Erickson, Douglas (*U.S.A.*)
Evans, Len (*Sydney, Australia*)

Feldman, Larry (*U.S.A.*)
Fenton, Colin, M.W.
Finch-Noyes, Tony
Fison, Sir Guy, M.W.
Flatt, Lloyd (*U.S.A.*)
Foley, Denis (*U.S.A.*)
Foulds, Stewart
Fourault, Yves (*Bordeaux*)
Fox, Percy, & Co.
Frescobaldi
Fronsac, les Gentilhommes de

Gibson, Victor (*Australia*)
Ginestet, Bernard (*Bordeaux*)
Ginestet, Pierre (*Bordeaux*)
Goldthorp, Anthony
Gordon-Clark, Guy
Grubb, Pat, M.W.

Hale, Ted, M.W.
Hallgarten, Fritz
Hallgarten, Dr. Peter
Hartung, W. (*Holland*)
Harveys of Bristol
Hasslacher, Peter
Haworth, the late Leslie
Healey, Ray (*Sydney, Australia*)
Hedges & Butler
Heidsieck, Jean-Marc (*Champagne*)
Hepworth, Anthony
Herf, Freiherr Ludwig (*Nahe*)
Heubleins (U.S.A.)
Heymann, Freddie
Heymann, the late Rudolf
Hill, Jack
Hill-Smith, Mark (*Yalumba, S. Australia*)
Hine, François (*Cognac*)
Hugel, Jean (*Alsace*)

Ichinose, Ben (*U.S.A.*)

Jaboulet, Paul (*Rhône*)
Jameson, Geoffrey, M.V.O., M.W.
Johnson, Hugh
Johnston, Nathaniel (*Bordeaux*)

Johnstone, Lt.-Col. Norman
Justerini & Brooks

Kenderman, Hans–Walter
Kerfoot, Dr. Thomas
von Kesselstatt (*Moselle*)
Kewley, Robert, M.W.
Kreeger, Harby (*U.S.A.*)
Kressman, Edouard (*Bordeaux*)
Kressmann, Yves (*Bordeaux*)
Krug, Paul (*Champagne*)

Lafite, Château
Lake, Dr. Max (*Sydney, Australia*)
Langenbach (London & Worms)
Lascelles, Giles
Latour, Château
Latour, Louis (*Burgundy*)
Lauerberg, Herr (*Moselle*)
Layton, T.A.
Lebègue & Co.
Leschallas, Anthony
Liehmann, Peter (*Barossa, Aus.*)
Lilburn, Ian
Ling, the late Archie
Littler, John
Littler, Timothy
Loeb & Co
Loudenne, Château
de Lur-Saluces, Comte Alexander
de Luze, Baron Geoffroy

Masters, Melvyn
Matuschka-Greiffenclau, Gräf and Gräfin
May, Fred
Miailhe, Jean (*Bordeaux*)
Miller, Tim
Milligan, David
Mondavi, Robert (*Napa, U.S.A.*)
Montgomery-Scott, Robert (*U.S.A.*)
Morrell, Peter J. (*New York*)
Mouton-Rothschild, Château
Müller, Rudolph (*Moselle*)

McDonnell, Kevin
McNally, Sandy (*U.S.A.*)
McWatters, George

Osborne, d'Arenberg (*S. Australia*)
Overton, Dr. Marvin (*U.S.A.*)

Palumbo, Peter
Pan, the late Pepe (*Jerez*)
Pardes, Yves (*Bordeaux*)
Parnell, Colin
Payne, Kerry (*U.S.A.*)
Penning-Rowsell, Edmund
Peppercorn, David, M.W.
Plumb, Professor J. H.
Pollock, David (*Ch. Latour*)
Ponnelle, Pierre (*Burgundy*)

Porter, Harold
Porter, John
Prade, Georges
Prats, Bruno (*Bordeaux*)
Pray, Sam (*France & U.S.A.*)
Price, Freddie
Purbrick, Eric (*Victoria, Australia*)

Quinton, Colin

Rausan-Ségla, Château
Reynier, Peter
Rhodes, Dr. Bernard L. (*U.S.A.*)
Ricasoli, Barone Bettino (*Italy*)
Riccardi, Count Riccardo (*Italy*)
Romanée Conti, Domaine de la
Roncarati, Dr. Bruno
de Rothschild, Baron Alain
de Rothschild, Baron Elie
de Rothschild, Baron Philippe
Rothschild, Lord
Roullet, Guy (*Cognac*)
Rutherford, David
Rutherford, Jack
Rutherford, Osborne & Perkin

Sakowitz, Robert (*U.S.A.*)
Sampson, Alistair
Sandeman, Tim
Schreiber, Mark
Schÿler, Guy (*Bordeaux*)
Scott, Ronald
Segan, Berek (*Melbourne, Australia*)
Serlis, Harry (*U.S.A.*)
Seyd, Leslie
Seysses, Jacques (*Burgundy*)
Sichel, Peter (*Bordeaux*)
Sichel, Walter
Simon, the late André
Skinner, Dr. Louis (*U.S.A.*)
Snell, John

Solci, Angelo (*Italy*)
Somerset, David
Spurrier, Steven (*Paris*)
Steyn, Gys (*S. Africa*)
Stirman, David (*U.S.A.*)
Strangman, Laurie

Talbot, Château
Tatham, Christopher, M.W.
Taylor, Bill & John (*S. Australia*)
Tesseron, Guy (*Bordeaux*)
Thanich, Dr. (Moselle)
Thoman, the late Gerhard
Thomson, Helen
Thorin, Jean (*Burgundy*)
Tinson, Harry (*Victoria, Australia*)
Tongue, R. E.
Trimbach, Hubert (*Alsace*)
Tyrrell, Murray (*Hunter Valley, Australia*)

Ungricht, Hugh (*Jerez*)

Vasselot, Marquis de (*France*)
Verlinden, Jan-Hein (*Holland*)
de Vilaine, Henri (*Burgundy*)
de Vogüé, Comte Alain (*Champagne*)

Walston, Lord
Waterhouse, Geoffrey
Waugh, Harry
Wente, the late Karl (*U.S.A.*)
Williams, the late Guy (*Jerez*)
Winton, Parry de
Witten, Dr. Victor (*U.S.A.*)
Woltner, the late Henri (*Bordeaux*)
Wyatt, Woodrow

Yapp, Robin

van Zeller, Fernando (*Oporto*)

The following very kindly helped with certain sections of the book:
Tony Alment and Christopher Holborow for casting their eyes over the senses of smell and taste
Peter A. Sichel for checking the French glossary
Dr. Peter Hallgarten for checking the German glossary
Count Riccardo Riccardi, Dr. Luigi Veronelli, and Dr. Bruno Roncarati for checking the Italian glossary
John Littler for advice on English Licensing Laws.

Index